# TITANIC
## In Picture Postcards

# TITANIC
## In Picture Postcards

Robert McDougall
and
Robin Gardiner

First published 2002

ISBN 0 7110 2896 6

Published by Ian Allan Publishing

an imprint of Ian Allan Publishing Ltd, Hersham, Surrey KT12 4RG.
Printed by Ian Allan Printing Ltd, Hersham, Surrey KT12 4RG.

Code: 0205/A2

**Author's Note**
Where ship names are given in the form *Celtic* 2 this means that the vessel concerned was the second of that name operated by the White Star Line.

**Picture Credits**
All the pictures reproduced in this book are from Robert McDougall's collection unless credited otherwise.

Pictures from Rembrandt are reproduced by kind permission of Philip Croucher of Rembrandt.

*Front cover:* White Star 'Olympic' class liners and two crew members from *Titanic*.

*Back cover:* More 'Olympics' with *Titanic* at bottom.

# CONTENTS

**WHITE STAR LINE**

**WHITE STAR**

OLYMPIC and TITANIC
Each 45,000 Tons

WHITE STAR LINE

**MAGAZINE**

The Sea, Ships, Ocean Travel
and
THE ORGAN OF THE WHITE STAR LINE

White Star Line's official magazine, the first published shortly before the *Titanic* disaster, proclaiming the entry into service of the new class of liner, and on page 126, a somewhat more restrained edition published shortly after the disaster.

# INTRODUCTION

The building of the 'Olympic' class of White Star liners, of which *Titanic* was the second of three, was the culmination of a series of vessels that had begun more than 30 years before. In 1867 the White Star Line, which had until then operated wooden sailing ships, predominantly on the Liverpool to Australia route, found itself in serious financial trouble. White Star was forced into liquidation, and its ships were sold off to meet its debts.

Under normal circumstances that would have been the end of the line, but waiting in the wings was Thomas Henry Ismay. Ismay already owned a couple of small sailing ships but wanted to move into the lucrative North Atlantic steamer trade. For the then not insubstantial sum of £1,000 Ismay bought the goodwill, name and famous house flag, a five-pointed white star on a red burgee, of the foundering White Star Line for his own company, T. H. Ismay & Co.

Not long afterwards Liverpool financier Gustavus Schwabe approached Ismay with an offer he could hardly refuse. Schwabe's nephew, Gustav Wolff, was in partnership with Edward Harland, who had a shipyard at Queen's Island, Belfast, and the financier had already invested heavily there. Schwabe, anxious to ensure a secure return on his investment, offered to finance Ismay's new line provided that all of its new vessels were constructed by Harland & Wolff on a cost plus profit basis. By the same agreement Harland & Wolff would not build ships for Ismay's competitors for the North Atlantic trade. The assured profits for the shipbuilders meant they would be able to build the best possible vessels for the White Star Line.

Edward Harland, the senior partner in the shipyard, had some revolutionary ideas about the design of passenger vessels but because he was generally building vessels for conservative and cost-conscious line owners he had never been able to put them into practice. Until then, first a hull had been built and then deckhouses were added, almost as an afterthought, to provide extra passenger accommodation. Harland wanted to build his ships with the extra passenger accommodation contained

**Thomas Henry Ismay, founder of O.S.N. Co who bought the White Star Line name, flag and goodwill in 1869, and built the company up into one of the foremost steamship lines in the world. *By kind permission of Philip Croucher of Rembrandt.***

within the hull, which would be continued upward higher than before. The new design would give a marked increase in passenger accommodation and comfort. Thomas Henry Ismay, who was nothing if not innovative, was impressed by Harland's ideas and promptly ordered three new vessels. Shortly afterwards the initial order was increased to four.

On 6 September 1869 the Oceanic Steam Navigation Company was registered with £400,000 of capital in 400 £1,000 shares. Thomas Henry Ismay owned 50 shares, his general manager George Hamilton Fletcher owned another 50, and Gustavus Schwabe had a dozen.

A little later Ismay took on a partner, William Imrie (Jnr). Ismay had met and become firm friends with Imrie while both of them were apprenticed to the shipbroking firm Imrie Tomlinson, between 1853 and 1856. When William Imrie (Snr), the senior partner in the shipbroking firm, died in 1870 his son William Imrie (Jnr) transferred the whole of his business to T. H. Ismay & Co. The company name was changed to Ismay, Imrie and Company.

On 27 August 1870, the first of the new ships, Harland & Wolff's Yard Number 73, *Oceanic*, was launched at Belfast. Because both Ismay and Harland believed that the workers in the Belfast shipyard would take more pride in building a ship that had a name, rather than just a yard number, all White Star ships were named when their keels were laid. This also meant that no christening ceremony was needed when the ships were launched.

Not surprisingly for so revolutionary a vessel (she has been described as 'the mother of modern liners') there were problems on the maiden voyage. By the time the ship was off Holyhead her engine bearings were overheating to the extent that she was obliged to put back to Liverpool for repair. The maiden voyage was resumed a fortnight later. This unfortunate tendency towards disappointing maiden voyages was to stay with White Star, and is one of the main reasons why the line is still so famous.

Over the next 30 years the Oceanic Steam Navigation Company prospered and never failed to pay its shareholders a premium, even though there were several price wars and other companies were unable to make a profit. Quite how this profit making came about has long been a source of conjecture but the recent discovery of tunnels at both the line's New York and Liverpool terminals suggests that not everybody, or everything, that crossed the Atlantic aboard White Star ships passed through customs or immigration control on either side of the Atlantic.

The *Oceanic* was soon followed into service by her sisters *Atlantic* and *Baltic*, and a little later, in February 1872 by the fourth, *Republic*, but they were not immediately successful. Regular travellers tended to stay with the lines they knew, such as the Cunard, Guion, Inman and National Lines.

The White Star Line's reputation for speed, comfort and reliability

*Left:* **Joseph Bruce Ismay, who took over control of White Star on his father's death in 1899, and sold it to American banker John Pierpont Morgan three years later.** *By kind permission of Philip Croucher of Rembrandt.*

*Below:* **Thomas Henry Ismay and his wife aboard a White Star liner sometime around 1880.**

steadily grew and more and more passengers sailed on its ships. It had always been Ismay's intention to establish a weekly service between Liverpool and New York; for this he needed five ships and so he ordered another two from Harland & Wolff, *Adriatic* (1) and *Celtic* (1). He optimistically believed he was about to have six; one more than he actually needed.

However, the following year, 1873, before the new ships had arrived from the builders, the White Star Line gained a dubious record: that of the worst Atlantic disaster then on record. The *Atlantic*, short of coal, and in appalling conditions, abandoned its run to Boston and instead made for Halifax. Approaching the safety of that port she ran ashore at Marr's Rock and broke up in the heavy seas with the loss of 588 lives. The ship was between 12 and 13 miles off course when she struck the rocks. *Atlantic* was equipped with 10 lifeboats capable of carrying about 600 people, less than half the ship's capacity, and about two-thirds of those on board at the time of the disaster. Dubious navigation and a somewhat cavalier attitude to passenger safety are two of the line's inclinations that have also ensured its lasting celebrity.

The first of the new two-funnelled steamers, *Britannic*, entered White Star service in June 1874. These new ships were larger and intended to be faster than the line's original four vessels, another tendency that would eventually end in tears with arguably the most famous shipping disaster in history. *Britannic's* sister ship,

*Germanic*, was delivered in May 1875. During the next year *Britannic* and *Germanic* both managed to capture the speed record for an Atlantic crossing. However, competition from the White Star Line's main rival, Cunard, was fierce and profits were down. Then things took a slight turn for the better when in 1877 the line, in company with Cunard, was awarded the Atlantic mail contract.

Thomas Ismay had three sons, Joseph Bruce, James and Bower. In 1880 Joseph Bruce entered the firm; he was 18 years old. J. Bruce, as he is generally known, was anything but his father's favourite son; that distinction fell on the second son James, but he was to have a longer and more influential stay with White Star than either his father or brothers. He became the White Star agent in New York in 1887, where he would complete his education as far as the day-to-day running of the line was concerned. The following year he married Florence Schieffelin, the daughter of a prominent New York banker.

J. Bruce and James both became partners in Ismay, Imrie & Co on 1 January 1891 and at the end of the year Thomas Henry Ismay resigned as manager. So as not to lose overall control T. H. Ismay retained his position as chairman of the company right up until his death, on 24 November 1899, when J. Bruce took the reins.

The management at Harland & Wolff also changed during the closing years of the 19th century. Edward Harland died in 1895 and with his demise William James Pirrie, who had become a partner in the firm 21 years before, became managing director.

**Joseph Bruce Ismay, flanked by his brothers James and Bower, on their daily inspection tour of the White Star Line's Liverpool landing stage.**

Pirrie, more than any other outsider, would have a tremendous influence on the destiny of the White Star Line.

The new supremo of the Oceanic Steam Navigation Company might have been quite proficient with the day-to-day running of the enterprise, but he was not an empire builder like his father. However, on the opposite side of the North Atlantic another empire builder was taking an interest in the White Star Line.

J. P. Morgan, possibly the most powerful banker the world has yet seen, had been fully occupied setting up and controlling various trusts, companies and groups of companies. His policy was to pay top price for any business he wanted, and then to group all the companies of any particular type together as combines. In this way, by late in the 19th century, he owned or controlled all of the railway rolling stock on the United States eastern seaboard, almost all of American steel production and most of the companies producing electricity and electrical goods, as well as numerous other enterprises. By the turn of the century Morgan was ready to add the transatlantic shipping companies to his empire.

First he bought the old Inman Line, which was renamed the American Line and formed the foundation of the International Marine Company. The old name was soon discarded as Morgan increased the capital from £3 million to £24 million and renamed the enterprise, the International Mercantile Marine Company, or I.M.M. as it was popularly known. Then he turned his attention to the other transatlantic passenger lines, snapping up the Atlantic Transport, Dominion, Leyland and Red Star Lines.

The big four Atlantic lines, North German Lloyds, Hamburg Amerika, Cunard and White Star, resisted Morgan's attempts to take them over. The German lines pretended to go along with his plans but in the breathing space gained acquired government backing to ensure their independence. Cunard did much the same thing, and managed to fight off Morgan's take-over bid with financial aid from the British government. For some reason the British government was not so helpful when it came to White Star.

At first Ismay, who controlled the Oceanic Steam Navigation Company (White Star), managed to persuade his shareholders that selling out to Morgan would not be in their best interests, but Morgan had a powerful ally in the White Star camp. Harland & Wolff was over-extended and having trouble raising enough money to complete vessels already under construction. The yard desperately needed an injection of capital, and Pirrie firmly believed that the best hope for his company's survival lay in the much larger assured market that would come with White Star's absorption into I.M.M. As it turned out he was right. He brought his considerable persuasive powers to bring I.M.M. and the White Star Line together, in the hope of acquiring working capital from Morgan.

In 1902 the Morgan combine offered the Oceanic Steam Navigation Company's shareholders 10 times that company's earnings for the year 1900. Now 1900 had been a very good year for O.S.N., many of whose vessels had been employed by the British government in transporting troops and supplies to South Africa, to fight the Boer War. The offer was worth £10,000,000 to the shareholders and it was too good for them to refuse. By 1 December 1902 the White Star Line belonged to J. P. Morgan's I.M.M. Company.

During negotiations the British government had belatedly expressed reservations about allowing the White Star fleet to fall into foreign hands, but an agreement that the ships would continue to sail under the British flag, use British officers and crews, and would be available to Britain in the event of a European war quelled the government's objections.

The agreement to sail the ships under the British flag and employ British crews was no great hardship for Morgan. Under American regulations in order for a ship to be eligible to fly the Stars and Stripes it had to be built in the United States, and none of the White Star ships had been. It was also very much cheaper to employ British officers and seamen than their American cousins. In fact it was much more economical to operate a British ship than an American one.

J. Bruce Ismay would become managing director and chairman of White Star under the new owners. Most of the other lines in the group would continue to operate as individual companies and retain their own management structures. The predictable result was that the individual lines that made up I.M.M. worked in direct competition with one another. Not surprisingly I.M.M. failed to show the sort of profits that Morgan was looking for, although the White Star Line under Ismay's direction continued to make money, but not enough to support the whole combine.

Even as the take-over was going ahead new ships were entering White Star service. They were the 'Big Four' class, then the biggest ships in the world, *Celtic* (2), *Cedric*, *Baltic* (2) and *Adriatic* (2). To maintain this lead, at least in size, the *Baltic* was lengthened by 20ft 6in during construction.

By 1904 I.M.M. was in crisis and Morgan was reluctant to support the combine any longer, unless a strong hand could be found to take control. The obvious choice was Joseph Bruce Ismay. Approaches were made to Ismay, who at first refused even to consider taking on the top job at I.M.M. However, an offer of £20,000 a year, a guarantee of absolute power within the company, an option to leave after six months' notice and a guarantee that Morgan would provide financial support for three years, finally persuaded him. Ismay accepted the position as President and Managing Director of the International Mercantile Marine Company. Under Ismay's direction the giant combine began to show a small profit.

In 1906 Gustav Wolff handed complete control of Harland & Wolff to Pirrie, who was confident that larger and larger ships would be needed by the White Star Line, and the rest of the I.M.M. group. Pirrie set about modernising the yard. Slipways 1, 2 and 3 were removed and replaced by just two much bigger ones. A huge steel gantry was constructed, more than 840ft long, 270ft wide and 185ft high, large enough to build the largest vessels Pirrie could imagine.

Then Cunard brought in its new 31,000-ton super-liners *Lusitania* and *Mauretania*, almost a third as big again as the 'Big Four', and with a top speed of around 26kt, about 10kt faster.

If the White Star Line was to prove once and for all that it was the premier passenger carrier something spectacular would have to be done. The time for the *Olympic* and her sister *Titanic* had come.

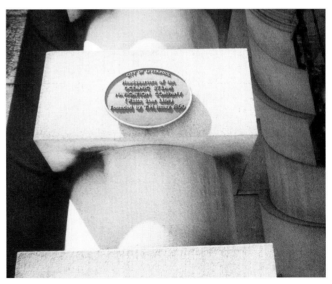

**Plaque outside the line's Liverpool headquarters today.**

*Left:* The White Star Line head offices at 30 James Street, Liverpool, soon after completion in 1900.

*Right:* The landing stage at Liverpool with the tender *Gallic*, bottom right. *Gallic* served at Cherbourg until the new tenders *Nomadic* and *Traffic*, specially built to service *Olympic*, *Titanic* and *Britannic*, entered service in 1911.

*Below:* The landing stage at Liverpool, the White Star Line's home port, with the liner *Majestic*, top right, and the Mersey tender *Magnetic*, tied up.

*Below Right:* The boat train from London's Euston Station at Liverpool in 1905. T. H. Ismay was a director of the London & North Western Railway Company, which brought transatlantic passengers from the capital to his vessels waiting in the River Mersey.

RIVERSIDE STATION, LIVERPOOL.

# THE 'OLYMPIC' CLASS

According to popular tradition, one night in 1907, J. Bruce Ismay and his wife Florence went to dine with James Pirrie and his wife at their London home, Downshire House, in Belgrave Square. It was at this dinner party that the idea of the 'Olympic' class of White Star liner, of which *Titanic* was the second, was supposedly conceived. The conversation between the two men would have centred around the design and delivery dates of the new ships. The plan was that the first two ships would be built side by side, one to be completed a few months before the other. Then a third would be built after the first two were in service, and their faults had shown up. By the end of that evening the 'Olympic' class liners were still only an idea but they were soon to become a reality.

By July 1908 the builders, under Pirrie's nephew Thomas Andrews, and his brother-in-law Alexander Carlisle, had produced a set of scale plans for the ships. The drawings were headed:

**400 Plan — 29 July 1908**
**(Proposed General Arrangement)**
S S No 400
850ft x 92ft x 64ft 6in
Design 'D'

Unlike the Cunard vessels, the new 'Olympics' were originally planned with two reciprocating engines instead of the relatively novel turbines. They were expected to return a speed of 21kt on these engines alone.

Initially the management of White Star simply would not believe in turbines until they had seen them in action for themselves, so they commissioned Harland & Wolff to build *Megantic* and *Laurentic*. *Megantic* was fitted with traditional reciprocating engines while the otherwise virtually identical *Laurentic* had a combination of turbine and reciprocating. The turbine-powered *Laurentic* would not be ready for her trials until well after construction of the first of the new 'Olympics' had begun. Although there was little difference in the overall top speed of the two vessels, *Laurentic* being slightly faster, there was a marked increase in fuel economy with the turbine-

powered vessel. The results of the trials persuaded the White Star Line and the builders that turbine engines had some merit, and it was decided to add one to each of the new liners.

To make sure that an adequate supply of steel and the specialised forgings required would be available from firms controlled by John Brown, and to gain access to the new technology involved in producing turbines, Harland & Wolff came to an agreement with the famous Clyde shipbuilders. Despite being direct competitors, the White Star and Cunard Lines had always been on relatively friendly terms. The agreement over the building of the turbine engines forged another link between the two lines inasmuch as John Brown was Cunard's favoured builder.

As well as being more opulent than either the *Lusitania* or the *Mauretania*, the new White Star liners were to be half as large again as the Cunard flagships. They were planned to be the largest man-made moving objects on earth.

The nominal chief designer at Harland & Wolff, the Honourable Alexander Carlisle, was nearing retirement and as a result the main design work was apparently carried out by Pirrie himself. Carlisle contented himself with mostly detail work such as decoration, fixtures and fittings, and the life-saving equipment. Originally he wanted 64 lifeboats but the numbers were reduced, against Carlisle's advice, first to 48, then 32 and finally to 16.

Eventually the plans for the first two of the new class of vessels were finalised. There only needed to be one complete set of drawings as it was intended that both ships would be identical at the time of their launch and could therefore be built from the same plans.

There were problems with the new service between Southampton and New York, however. The American port did not have any piers long enough to accommodate the new liners, and the same applied to the two other regular ports of call on the Atlantic route, Cherbourg and Queenstown. Eventually the Americans were persuaded to improve the facilities at New York, but at the French and Irish ports passengers, baggage and mail would have to be ferried to and from the ships in tenders.

## Design of the *Titanic*

In order to understand events aboard *Titanic* on the night of 14/15 April 1912, a brief description of the 'Olympic' class ships might be useful. As finally planned they were to be 882ft 6in long and 92ft 6in wide. They were to measure 45,324 gross registered tons but displace (actual all-up weight) about 66,000 tons.

Work began on Yard Number 400, *Olympic*, on 16 December 1908 and three and a half months later, on 31 March 1909, the second monster vessel was begun alongside the first. Together they would grow over the coming months; the first one of the most successful liners in history, the second probably the least successful.

By mid-April 1910 the hull of *Olympic* had been plated. To keep the number of joints to a minimum large steel plates about 30ft long, 6ft wide and 1in thick were used wherever possible. The plates were fixed to frames, mostly made of 10in steel channel, spaced 3ft apart over the hull's mid-section, 2ft apart at her bow and 27in apart at the stern. The structural steel of the ship was, in the main, hydraulically riveted together for extra strength, as was the hull plating, a relatively new process at the

*Left:* Lord Pirrie, Managing Director of Harland & Wolff which built *Titanic*, on the left, and Captain E. J. Smith who brought about the destruction of the vessel, on the right.

*Below:* During construction of the first 'Olympics' the White Star Line had two other ships, very similar to one another, built to test the efficiency of turbine engines. The first of these vessels, fitted with two traditional quadruple-expansion reciprocating engines, was the *Megantic*, originally laid down for the Dominion Line as the *Albany*.

time. This was about the only new procedure or idea employed in the construction of these ships. Obviously, considerable force would have to be applied to the outer skin of the vessel to disturb these heavy-duty frames seriously, especially at the forward end of the ship.

The vessels were fitted with a double bottom, with a 5ft 3in gap between the inner and outer skins. This double bottom was subdivided into 73 separate trimming tanks which could hold almost 4,500 tons of water ballast, so as to ensure that the ship floated in an upright attitude. Enough, one would have thought, to correct any slight tendency the vessel might have towards listing to one side or the other under all normal circumstances, but one would be wrong, as we shall see.

The hull was subdivided into 16 separate compartments by 15 transverse bulkheads, each $\frac{1}{2}$in thick, which reached, in most cases, to well above the water line. The bulkhead between boiler rooms 4 and 5 was exceptional in that it reached only a mere $2\frac{1}{2}$ft above the waterline. On the lower decks the bulkheads were fitted with automatic watertight doors to allow communication between the

*Top:* From left to right, Alexander Carlisle who was instrumental in designing the 'Olympic' class ships, Captain E. J. Smith, who commanded first *Olympic* and then *Titanic*, and J. Bruce Ismay, who ordered the construction of the vessels.

*Above:* The second vessel built to test turbine engines was the *Laurentic*, fitted with two triple-expansion reciprocating engines and one low pressure turbine. This ship was originally laid down for the Dominion Line as the *Alberta* and although little, or no, faster than *Megantic* she was more economical to operate.

boiler and engine rooms, which would close immediately if water entered the ship. They could also be closed by simply flicking a switch on the bridge.

The bulkheads were positioned so as to enable the vessel to remain afloat with any two major compartments flooded. The ship could also remain afloat with the four forward compartments flooded, which was only likely to happen if she rammed something or went hard aground. If the vessel was itself rammed, the worst that was expected was the opening of two compartments to the sea. The bulkheads between the boiler rooms were backed by coal bunkers which again ran the full width of the ship.

Bulkheads 2, 3 and 4, numbering from the bow, were pierced by a watertight passageway on the lowest deck of the vessel (tank top). This passageway was protected at each end by watertight doors. At its nearest point to the outer skin of the ship it came within 5ft 3in of the bottom plating and about 16ft from the plating of the hull side. This 'firemen's passage', as it was known, presents a major problem when dealing with the collision which supposedly sank *Titanic*.

The 'Olympic' class ships had 10 steel decks. The uppermost or boat deck had no passenger accommodation, but the senior officers' cabins were situated at the forward end immediately behind the bridge. The wireless room was about 20yd back on the port side of this block of cabins, known to the crew as the officer's house. The Marconi Company, which supplied the wireless, guaranteed it a range of 350 miles.

As can be gathered from the name, most of the ship's boats were kept on this boat deck: 16 wooden lifeboats under davits and two collapsible boats, C and D, resting on the deck just inboard of forward Boats 1 and 2. Two more collapsible boats, A and B, were kept on top of the officers' cabins on either side of the forward funnel where they would be all but useless in an emergency. Boats 1 and 2, only 25ft long compared to the 30ft of the other wooden lifeboats, were emergency boats, which were kept swung out while the ship was at sea. In total the first two 'Olympic' class vessels had lifeboats for 1,178 persons each.

As well as the lifeboats the ships carried 3,560 lifejackets, 13 more than the total number of persons who could be transported.

There were also 48 traditional circular red and white lifebuoys, six of which were fitted with an electric light which illuminated when the lifebuoy entered the water.

Besides devices intended to increase the chances of survival for those already in the water, the ships were equipped with a variety of apparatus to summon assistance before the vessel might be in danger of sinking. Pyrotechnic signalling arrangements included 36 mortar-like signals with a firing socket on either side of the bridge, 12 ordinary rockets, two Manwell Holmes deck flares and 12 blue lights.

The open areas of the 500ft-long boat deck were devoted to promenade space for officers at the forward end, first class passengers amidships, then engineers, and second class at the rear end.

The next deck, descending, was A deck, which was entirely devoted to the use of first class passengers. Both first class entrances with their grand staircases and lifts and the Verandah and Palm Court restaurants, the first class smoking room and the lounge were all here, along with about 30 staterooms.

B deck supposedly differed on *Titanic* from that originally fitted to *Olympic*. Common to both ships was the entirely first class cabin space, second class smoking

*Left:* **A cross-section of the *Olympic*. *Titanic* would have appeared to be identical except for B deck, which was supposedly cabin space where this illustration shows promenade. Indications are that *Titanic*'s conversion was never completed, if it was ever begun.**

room and restaurant. On *Olympic* the outer edges of B deck were promenade areas. On *Titanic* this area was supposedly converted into cabins and suites reaching right out to the sides of the ship. Where the starboard side second class promenade was sited on *Olympic*, *Titanic* apparently had the pavement café, the Café Parisien.

C deck was entirely devoted to first class cabin space amidships, with the second class library just aft. The aft well deck was promenade space for third class and on the aft part of the deck, beneath the poop deck, were the third class public rooms. At the forward end of this deck in the forecastle were situated the crew's galley and messes, the crew hospital and carpenter's shop. The rest of the forecastle at this level was machinery space.

D deck amidships was again first class, with the dining saloon, reception rooms and cabins. Further aft were the first and second class galley, sculleries, hospital, pantries, butchers and bakers. Next came the second class dining saloon and then second class cabins. The extreme rear of the deck was third class accommodation. The forward end of the deck immediately in front of and below the bridge was the third class open space. In the bow were firemen's quarters and stores.

E deck was mixed accommodation with trimmers and seamen forward, third class aft of them. Then came first class in the forward part of its midships section, followed by second class. Bringing up the rear, as usual, came third class.

F deck, deep within the ship, was mostly third class. At the extreme bow end came firemen's quarters, then a large number of third class cabins. The midships areas of F deck contained one of the first swimming baths afloat, third class dining saloon and engineers' accommodation. Further aft were second class cabins and right in the extreme stern came third class, again.

G deck had crew quarters forward followed by third class open berths (hammock space), first class baggage rooms, then the post office and squash court. The whole midships section of this deck was taken up by coal bunkers, boiler casings, engine casings and store rooms. Aft of this area came second class cabins and bringing up the rear, more third class, in this case not permanent. This third class area could be made to double as cargo space.

Forward on the next deck down, the orlop deck, was cargo space and the mail room. The centre section was again devoted to boiler casings, coal bunkers and the tops of the huge engines. Aft of these came the refrigerated cargo rooms, store rooms and the aft cargo hold.

On the lowest deck, the tank top, were the main engine rooms; these actually reached up three decks. Next aft was the turbine engine room. Then came the four electric dynamos which produced the power to drive all the cranes and winches, the lights, the heaters, the gymnasium machinery, first and second class lifts and all the other electrical equipment aboard. In addition to the main dynamos there were two emergency generators situated on D deck, adjacent to the after boiler casing.

Forward of the main engine room were the six huge boiler rooms.

Each vessel had a total of 29 boilers, fired by 159 furnaces. Number 6 boiler room was situated where the vessel's hull began to narrow towards the bow.

On this, the lowest deck regularly occupied by members of the crew, and in the space created by the double bottom of the vessel, were the inlets for the exceptional number of pumps aboard. There were no less than 124 of these intakes, ranging in size from 3in to 18in in diameter, spread throughout the lowest levels of the ship. All of these pumps were interconnected by 10in-diameter pipes. The ability of these vessels to pump water overboard was very impressive indeed.

The main engines were capable of producing 15,000hp apiece and the turbine turned out a further 16,000hp.

In October 1910, the *Olympic* was ready for launching and on the 20th of that month, especially painted white for the benefit of photographers, slid stern first into the River Laggan. Fitting out would take just over seven months. In that time the boilers were installed along with the masts, which towered 200ft above the waterline, and four enormous funnels, only 55ft shorter.

The ornate first class cabins were fitted out with all the care normally reserved for stately homes. The interiors of the public rooms were panelled and painted, carpets were laid and machinery installed. The installation of more than 200 miles of cable was required to feed power to all the electrical fixtures and fittings, including more than 10,000 light bulbs.

On 29 May 1911, *Olympic* began her two days of sea trials, which went off without any serious problems. She was handed over to her owners, with full ceremony, in a brilliant example of Edwardian media management, on the 31st. That selfsame day the second leviathan was launched.

At about 4.30pm, *Olympic* left Belfast for Liverpool where she was to be opened for public inspection for one day. She departed the Merseyside port on the evening of 1 June for Southampton to prepare for her maiden voyage under the Commodore of the White Star fleet, Captain Edward John Smith, who had taken command the day before.

On 14 June 1911, *Olympic* left Southampton for New York, via Queenstown in Ireland, on her maiden voyage. She completed the journey at an average speed of 21.17kt, entering New York harbour at 7.45am on 21 June, after an uneventful passage. During the last few moments of docking *Olympic* had a minor accident when she backed into and almost sank the tug *O.L. Halenbeck*.

Nor was it Captain Smith's first accident. Over the previous 22 years he had run *Republic (1)*, *Coptic* and *Adriatic (2)* aground, suffered fires aboard *Majestic (1)* and *Baltic (2)*, and had a boiler explosion aboard *Republic (1)* that killed three men and injured seven more. And Captain Smith's career was by no means over yet. As a result of experience gained from *Olympic*'s maiden voyage some small alterations were ordered for *Titanic*. Most noticeable among these was the enclosure of the forward end of A deck, which was carried out only during the final week of *Titanic*'s construction. If testimony given later is to be believed, planned alterations to B deck were never completed.

## Preparing to Sail

On 20 September 1911 an incident occurred that I believe set in motion a chain of events that would lead to the loss of the *Titanic*. As *Olympic*, with Captain E. J. Smith and the harbour pilot George William Bowyer on the bridge, was leaving Southampton Water at the start of her fifth westbound Atlantic crossing she was rammed in the starboard quarter by the Royal Navy's armoured cruiser HMS *Hawke*, captained by Commander William Frederick Blunt.

The cruiser's armoured bow tore a huge hole in the relatively soft side of the liner, putting *Olympic's* starboard main and central turbine engines out of action at the same time. On the following day *Olympic* crept back to Southampton, where the damage to her hull and machinery was inspected. The starboard propeller, and its shafting, were so badly damaged that this would have to be replaced once the damaged liner could be returned to the builders in Belfast, to the only dry-dock in the world large enough to take her. Before she could even attempt the voyage, a full week's work was needed to patch the huge hole in her hull temporarily.

On the trip back to Belfast *Olympic* could use only her port main engine and was obliged to steam at about 10kt. The turbine engine, which ran on exhaust steam from both, or either, main engines was inoperable, indicating that the damage inflicted by *Hawke* extended deeply enough into the liner to have put the turbine, situated on the centre line of the ship, out of action. In light of this, the owner's claim that the cruiser's bow had penetrated *Olympic's* hull only to a depth of about 8ft seems unlikely.

Two months after the *Hawke* incident, at about 4.00pm on 20 November 1911, after a day supposedly spent testing machinery and adjusting compasses, a vessel bearing the name *Olympic* quietly slipped out of Belfast. Had that vessel really been *Olympic* there would have been no reason to adjust compasses that had been set only a couple of months earlier, nor to test machinery that had already satisfactorily completed four Atlantic crossings. In the time the liner had been out of service she had cost White Star more than £250,000 in repairs and lost fares, a powerful incentive to do something, anything, to restore the company's income.

*Olympic's* **second return to the builders occurred in early March 1912 after she lost a port main propeller blade in a collision with a submerged wreck somewhere off the Grand Banks, Newfoundland.**

In the last few weeks prior to *Olympic's* departure from the Irish shipyard rumour that she had been switched with her sister *Titanic* was rife. The owners and builders denied the switch and the shipyard workers, if they wanted to keep their jobs, had to accept that denial whether they believed it or not.

If the rumours were true, and they would flare up again four months later, then the vessel which slipped out of Belfast in the gathering gloom of that late November afternoon was really the mechanically completed, but not entirely fitted out, Number 401 *Titanic*, and not Number 400 *Olympic*. The liner reached Southampton on the morning of the 22nd.

On All Fools' Day 1912, as the ship now known as *Titanic* was preparing for her acceptance trials at Belfast, fire reportedly broke out in her Number 10 bunker, at the forward end of Number 5 boiler room. The fire was still burning brightly when at 6.00 the following morning the ship began what have been ludicrously described as her 'trials', which lasted a short working day, half of which was spent in a leisurely cruise up and down Belfast Lough. Aboard the ship were Harold Sanderson, representing the White Star Line, Thomas Andrews, the managing director of Harland & Wolff and James Pirrie's nephew, and Captain E. J. Smith in command.

After the so-called 'trials' *Titanic* headed directly for Southampton, without being opened to the public at Liverpool as her sister had been. Public inspection of the ship would also be denied at the Hampshire port. On the short voyage down from the builders the apparently brand-new ship, with her engines not even partially run in, exceeded her sister's previous best speed by more than 1kt.

*Titanic* was due to sail on her maiden voyage on the 10th, and there was a lot of work still to do if she was to be ready. Cabins were not properly fitted out, carpets were still to be laid, equipment had to be checked, coal had to be brought aboard, and worst of all, the ship was on fire. Why on earth would the White Star Line accept a ship from the builders with a fire raging in one of her forward bunkers? A fire that could, and should, have been dealt with at Belfast before the 'trials' had even begun.

Because of a major coal strike that had been going on since early January harbours around Britain were crowded with ships that, once they had arrived, were unable to collect enough coal to leave again. *Olympic*, because of the coal shortage, had topped up her bunkers in America, and ostensibly by carrying extra fuel in unoccupied cabins, had managed to squeeze almost, but not quite, enough aboard to complete the round voyage back to New York. She had left Southampton only hours before *Titanic* arrived there, taking with her most of what small coal reserves existed.

Five other I.M.M. ships laid up in Southampton were stripped bare of fuel, not one of them having enough to proceed to sea themselves, in order to fill *Titanic's* bunkers. Then, in an act of unimaginable stupidity, Captain E. J. Smith allowed tons of precious coal to be poured into *Titanic's* already burning bunker. As any schoolboy knows, heated coal gives off explosive coal gas (mostly hydrogen), which requires only a spark to ignite it. Why had Captain Smith turned the bunker into a huge bomb that could go off at any moment?

At about the same time that *Titanic* was heading for Southampton, orders to put to sea were on their way to another I.M.M. vessel, in London. The Leyland Line cargo passenger ship *Californian*, like so many other vessels, had apparently been stranded in port for want of coal, with a nondescript cargo in her holds, but when her orders to put to sea arrived the coal problem suddenly disappeared. The wireless operator, Cyril Evans, was sent ashore to pick up a wireless chart for the North Atlantic, which would tell him when it was possible to contact other ships at sea. In his haste Evans grabbed the chart for the South Atlantic in error and only when he had returned to *Californian* did he discover his mistake. *Californian's* master, Captain Stanley Lord, in his hurry to get his ship under way, could not spare the time to allow Evans to go back for the correct chart. He would just have to do the best he could without the chart's assistance. Despite the numbers of would-be travellers desperately searching for a berth aboard anything that might get them to America, Captain Lord could not wait to take on fare-paying passengers. *Californian* departed London on 5 April 1912 and headed for her rendezvous with destiny at a steady 10kt or 11kt, her best speed. Perhaps it should be mentioned here that Captain Lord held a rather unusual record: that of disembarking and embarking, at sea, more people and horses in a given time than any other captain afloat.

On the other side of the 'Pond', at New York, other preparations were under way. The Cunard liner *Carpathia*, which curiously does not appear on the company's 1912 schedule list from January until 18 April, was also preparing for sea. The Cunarder had arrived in New York in late March but instead of remaining tied up at her usual berth at Pier 54 she spent some time, away from prying eyes, fitting out in the Brooklyn Navy Yard. Before *Carpathia* was due to sail on 11 April additional provisions, blankets and bedding were put aboard, and six extra doctors joined the ship for the forthcoming voyage. Normally *Carpathia* carried only one doctor, Dr J. E. Kemp. The extra physicians were Dr Frank McGee (English), Dr Gottlieb Rencher (American), Dr Lengil Arpad (Hungarian), Dr F. Blackmarr (American), Dr Henry F. Bauenthal (American) and a so far unnamed Italian doctor. Obviously some sort of medical emergency was anticipated.

*Above:* **The third of the 'Olympic' class, *Britannic*, on the stocks.**

*Below:* **The second of the 'Olympic' class ships, *Titanic*, here seen at Southampton prior to her maiden, and only, voyage.**

*Above:* There were three ships in the 'Olympic' class, the first built being *Olympic* itself. Here she is seen at Liverpool immediately after leaving the builders and before proceeding to Southampton to prepare for her maiden voyage.

*Below: Britannic,* sliding into the River Laggan at Belfast.

*Right: Britannic* as she never appeared in life. Before completion *Britannic* was taken over by the British government for war service as a hospital ship. She struck a mine and sank in the Aegean Sea on 21 November 1916.

*Below right:* The harbour at Belfast, looking westwards, with Harland & Wolff's shipyard at top right.

R.M.S. Britannic

Length, 900 ft.
Breadth, 94 ft.
Tonnage, 50,000

THE HARBOUR, FROM QUEENS BRIDGE, BELFAST

SHIPBUILDING GANTRIES,
HARLAND & WOLFF'S SHIPYARDS, BELF

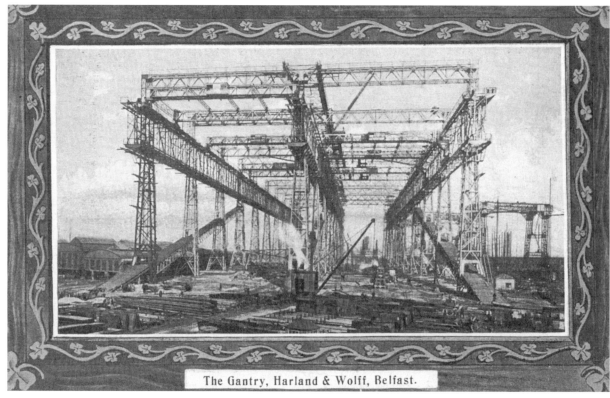

The Gantry, Harland & Wolff, Belfast.

*Left:* Harland & Wolff's shipyard at Queen's Island, Belfast, showing the array of cranes and the special gantry erected for the construction of *Olympic* and *Titanic* at the extreme right.

*Below left:* A view of the special gantry at Harland & Wolff constructed to facilitate building of the 'Olympic' class vessels.

*Right:* Another view of the 'Arrol' gantry at Belfast, giving some idea of the immense size.

*Below:* The 'Arrol' gantry seen from the River Laggan. Viewed from this end, *Olympic* was built on the left-hand slipway, and *Titanic* on the right.

HARLAND & WOLFF'S SHIPBUILDING YARD, BELFAST.

The Great Gantry, Harland & Wolff's, Shipyard, Belfast

Entrance to Belfast Harbour.

*Above:* Belfast Harbour with the Thompson dry-dock in the left foreground and the gantry where *Olympic, Titanic* and *Britannic* were built, a little further away.

*Left:* The first of the sisters under construction. Here the bottom of the hull is almost complete prior to fitting the lowest deck in the ship, the tank top, and erecting the frames forming the vessel's skeleton.

*Above right: Olympic,* on the right, nears launch day, her hull painted white to aid photographers who would be on hand to record the event.

*Right: Olympic* on launch day, 20 October 1910. In the background, with most of the scaffolding removed, *Titanic's* fully plated hull can clearly be seen.

*Left: Olympic* slides backwards into the River Laggan. She was launched on 20 October 1910 and then towed to the fitting-out quay to have her boilers and other mechanical equipment installed.

*Below:* The first class smoking room. While *Olympic* was at the fitting-out quay, work on her passenger accommodation began. First class public rooms and cabins were fitted and decorated to a standard that would not have disgraced the world's best hotels. *Titanic's* interior decoration was very similar to that of *Olympic* only more lavish, with carpets where her sister only had floor tiles.

*Right:* The first class restaurant on *Olympic.*

*Below right:* The first class dining saloon on *Olympic,* showing the great size of some of the public rooms aboard these vessels.

*Left: Olympic's Verandah Café, where, on Titanic, Mr Gatti's staff were to wait on wealthy passengers' every wish.*

*Below left:* Some of the 9,000 men who built *Olympic*, *Titanic* and *Britannic*.

*Right: Titanic* on the morning of 31 May 1911, shortly before launching.

*Below:* Before *Titanic* could slide backwards into the River Laggan there was a great deal of last-minute work to do such as greasing the slipway and removing timber props. During this phase of the launch proceedings one man was crushed and later died.

*Left:* Despite accidents *Titanic's* launch went ahead, and with hardly a ripple she slid into the water at midday.

*Below left: Titanic* immediately after launching and before being towed to the fitting-out quay.

*Above:* A boiler going aboard an 'Olympic' class ship, probably *Britannic*. The difficulty in determining which ship is which is demonstrated here as this vessel, on close examination, shows characteristics of all three.

*Left: Titanic* fitting out in the Thompson Graving Dock, then the largest dry-dock in the world.

*Above:* Reconstruction of a second class bedroom on *Titanic*.

*Left:* A bed as found in second class cabins on *Titanic*.

*Left:* Not looking her best, *Titanic* with all four funnels erected but unpainted.

*Right:* Guglielmo Marconi who is erroneously credited with inventing wireless. *Olympic* and *Titanic* were fitted with the most powerful wireless equipment produced by the Marconi Company.

*Below: Titanic* in March 1912, nearing completion.

# HANDS ACROSS THE SEA

WHITE STAR LINE

TITANIC

IN·SPITE·OF·HALF·A·WORLD·BETWEEN
I·CHERISH·YOU·IN·MEMORY,
AND·LOVE·TO·KEEP·OUR·FRIENDSHIP·GREEN,
WITH·HANDS·ACROSS·THE·SEA.

WHITE STAR LINE
OLYMPIC & TITANIC

THIRD CLASS
ACCOMMODATION

THE LARGEST STEAMERS IN THE WORLD

*Left:* To celebrate the commencement of a weekly service between Southampton and New York by the new 'Olympics' the White Star Line produced this 'Hands Across The Sea' card featuring a representation of *Titanic*.

*Right:* An Irish advertisement for the new White Star leviathans, showing *Olympic*. Although *Titanic* was reputedly a thousand tons heavier than her sister, both ships are credited with exactly the same tonnage in this advertisement.

*Below left:* An unusual advertisement for *Olympic* and *Titanic*, the largest steamers in the world, pointing out that they catered for third class passengers. The vessel shown is *Olympic*.

**White Star Line**

**Europe to America.**

*Left:* A White Star and L&NWR advertisement for the shipping line's Liverpool to America route. The vessel shown is *Olympic*, which was too large to operate out of Liverpool and was in fact working between Southampton and New York, with stops at Cherbourg in France and Queenstown (now Cobh) in Southern Ireland.

*Right:* Cards produced by the most reputable of companies purported to show *Titanic*. This card by Raphael Tuck shows *Olympic*.

*Below right:* The White Star Line began to advertise the new super-liners *Olympic* and *Titanic* before they actually entered service. Postcard manufacturers, unable to obtain pictures of *Titanic*, happily substituted *Olympic*.

*Olympic*
again stands
in for *Titanic*
in this colour
card by Tuck.

### R. M. S. "OLYMPIC".

45,000 tons gross register.  66,000 tons displacement.  Built by Harland & Wolff, Belfast; launched October 20, 1910.
Accommodation 2,500 passengers and a crew of 860.  Speed 21 knots.  Estimated cost £ 1,500,000.
The following are the dimensions, etc., of the great vessel:

| | | | |
|---|---|---|---|
| Length over all . . . . | 882ft. 6in. | Height of funnels above | Number of water-tight bulkheads  15 |
| Breadth over all . . . . | 92ft. 6in. | casing . . . . . . . 72ft. 0in. | Rudder weights . . . . 100 tons. |
| Breadth over boat deck  . | 94ft. 0in. | Height of funnels above boat | Stern frame, rudder and |
| Height from bottom of keel | | deck . . . . . . . 81ft. 6in. | brackets . . . . . . 280 tons. |
| to boat deck . . . . | 97ft. 4in. | Distance from top of funnel | Each anchor . . . . . 15 tons. |
| Height from bottom of keel | | to keel . . . . . . 175ft. 0in. | Bronze Propeller . . . 22 tons. |
| to top of captain's house | 105ft. 7in. | Number of steel decks . . . . 11 | Launching weight . . 27,000 tons. |

R.M.S. Olympic

*Left: Olympic* as herself with a comprehensive description of the vessel's outstanding features, all of which would have applied equally well to *Titanic* with the single exception of the gross registered tonnage.

*Below left: Olympic* early in her career. The picture has been artistically improved by the addition of smoke issuing from the aft funnel. This funnel was not in fact connected to any of the boiler flues but merely provided ventilation to the engine and boiler rooms.

*Right:* Card issued by Thomas Cook & Son, travel agents, showing *Olympic* and advertising travel aboard both of White Star's new liners. *By kind permission of Philip Croucher of Rembrandt.*

WHITE STAR LINE.

"OLYMPIC." 45,000 TONS.

AND

"TITANIC." 45,000 TONS.

THE LARGEST STEAMERS IN THE WORLD.

To NEW YORK,
From SOUTHAMPTON-CHERBOURG-QUEENSTOWN.
From LIVERPOOL-QUEENSTOWN.

To BOSTON,
From LIVERPOOL-QUEENSTOWN.

For Freight and Passage apply to

THOS. COOK & SON,
31, Fargate, SHEFFIELD;
16, Clumber Street and
97, Derby Road, NOTTINGHAM;
and Gallowtree Gate, LEICESTER.

R·M·S· OLYMPIC

WIRELESS TELEGRAPHY

OLYMPIC

*Left:* The same picture of *Olympic* as used in the Thomas Cook card but in this slightly later rendition, produced after *Titanic* had sunk, only the vessel's correct name appears. The part played by wireless in the rescue of *Titanic* survivors is acknowledged by the added text showing that *Olympic* was also equipped with 'Wireless Telegraphy'.

*Below:* A sepia advertising card for both *Olympic* and *Titanic*, again showing the class leader.

*Above right:* An official White Star card advertising *Olympic* and *Titanic*, featuring the former at left and *Titanic* in the distance, bottom right.

*Below right: Olympic* soon after leaving Southampton, early in her career.

The Largest and Finest Steamers in the world
WHITE STAR LINE
"OLYMPIC"          ✪          "TITANIC"
882½ FEET LONG          45,000 TONS REGISTER          92½ FEET BROAD

White Star Line

R.M.S. Olympic

WHITE STAR
LINE

TRIPLE-SCREW R.M.S. "OLYMPIC."
46,439 TONS.

*Above left: Olympic* dropping off a harbour pilot.

*Left: Olympic* at speed in this post-*Titanic* disaster official White Star colour card.

*Above: Olympic* again representing both herself and *Titanic* on an official White Star card.

*Right:* White Star advertisement showing some of the various types of vessel operated by the line. *Titanic* and *Olympic* are represented at centre and bottom.

43

S.S.OLYMPIC.

*Above and opposite page:* A three-picture series showing *Titanic* assisted by tugs, leaving the builders, on her way towards Belfast Lough and on the Irish Sea on 3 April 1912.

"OLYMPIC" & "TITANIC"
THE LARGEST STEAMERS IN THE WORLD
WHITE STAR LINE
WHITE STAR LINE
SOUTHAMPTON · CHE
LIVERPOOL TO
LONDON TO
NEW YORK
AGENTS:-
James Scott & Co, Queenstow

*Left:* White Star advertisement and calendar for 1912 displayed on the premises of its Queenstown agents, James Scott and Company.

*Below: Olympic* as herself with the name on the bow in oversize letters.

S. S. Olympic.

OLYMPIC

*Above: Titanic* departing
Belfast on 3 April 1912.
*By kind permission of
Philip Croucher of
Rembrandt.*

*Right:* On *Titanic's* bridge
as she steams through
Belfast Lough was Captain
Edward John Smith,
known to his officers as
'E.J.' He is seen here
aboard his previous
command, *Olympic*.

*Left:* Captain Smith with his dog; supposedly an Irish wolfhound. *By kind permission of Philip Croucher of Rembrandt.*

*Below:* Captain Smith, seated, with his wife, Eleanor, behind him and his daughter, Helen, seated on the deck in front.

536. CHERBOURG
« L'OLYMPIC », de la White Star Line (50.000 Tonnes)
partant pour New-York (leaving for New-York)
(Le plus grand transatlantique Anglais)

Le Goubey. Édit., St-Pierre-Eglise

200 CHERBOURG. — Le Transatlantique « Olimpic » de la White Star Line, 45.000 tonnes,
vitesse 21 nœuds, longueur 258 m., largeur 28 m., profondeur 29 m. 50. — LL.

*Top and above:* On her way to New York *Olympic*, like *Titanic* a few days later, would first call at Cherbourg.

*Left:* Even as *Titanic* was approaching Southampton, *Olympic* was leaving for New York.

*Below: Olympic* at New York.

# THE VOYAGE BEGINS

Captain Smith arrived aboard *Titanic* at about 7.30am on 10 April 1912 and went straight to his cabin. Chief Officer Henry Tingle Wilde, whose job it was to sort out any problems and prepare the ship for sea, was awaiting him there.

Wilde had joined *Titanic*, against his will, only that morning. Previously he had occupied the same position aboard *Olympic*. Command of *Olympic* had passed to Captain Herbert James Haddock, White Star's youngest captain. Wilde's transfer to *Titanic* had meant a reshuffle amongst the ship's senior officers. The existing Chief Officer, William McMaster Murdoch, was downgraded to First Officer. Charles Herbert Lightoller was moved down from First to Second Officer. David Blair, who had been Second Officer, left the ship altogether. Before doing so he had the lookouts' binoculars removed from the crow's nest and placed in his cabin.

The rest of the bridge officers stayed in their expected posts with Herbert Pitman as Third Officer, Joseph Groves Boxhall at Fourth, Harold Godfrey Lowe at Fifth and James Moody as Sixth Officer. With the exception of Wilde the officers had all joined the ship while she was still in Belfast. The new Chief Officer had apparently never set foot on *Titanic* before the morning she was to sail, but soon after joining the ship he wrote to his sister saying '. . . I still don't like this ship . . .' How could Mr Wilde 'still' dislike a ship he had never even set eyes on until the morning he sailed aboard her? The letter was amongst those that would leave the ship at Queenstown.

Meanwhile the rest of the crew were coming aboard. With so many ships and their crews lying idle, the White Star Line should have been able to assemble a hand-picked crew. Some of the men signed on had served aboard *Olympic*, and knew their way about the liners, but many more had not and would need several days to acclimatise themselves. Because of the fire, which still burned merrily in Bunker 10, a dozen extra firemen were drafted aboard from *Oceanic*, which was inactive for want of coal, to deal with it.

The lookouts' job, which entailed working two hours on and four off, was considered to be a 'cushy number', so there would have

been no shortage of applications from qualified men. Normally White Star only took on lookouts who had recently passed an eye test, but for this voyage it made an exception.

Not all of the crew were White Star employees. Most of the catering staff for the à la carte restaurant worked for Gatti's fashionable London restaurant. The ship's two wireless operators John (Jack) Phillips and Harold Sidney Bride were employed by the Marconi Company. The ship's post office was operated by three employees of the American postal service and two from the Royal Mail.

At about the same time that Captain Smith boarded the ship, so did Captain Maurice Harvey Clarke, an Assistant Immigration Officer for the Board of Trade. Clarke was there to inspect the ship to ensure that it was fit to carry emigrants across the Atlantic. He was well known to *Titanic's* senior officers for his meticulous approach to his job. He was regarded as a pain in the neck who would allow nothing to pass unchecked. On the morning of 10 April 1912 he inspected the passenger accommodation and insisted that two lifeboats were lowered. He also apparently checked the documents of every member of the crew. (This seemingly trivial detail assumes greater importance later in the story.) Somehow, the 'pain in the neck' failed to notice the smoke issuing from Number 10 bunker.

Between 9.30am and 11.00am the third class passengers were herded aboard through the aft entrance on C deck and the forward entrance on D deck. These passengers were sorted into 'immigrants' and 'steerage' (steerage being the cheapest berths aboard) and given a quick medical inspection. The company did not want to transport anyone across the Atlantic just to be told that they were too mangy to be allowed into America, which would mean that it would have to transport them all the way back at its own expense.

Just before 11.30am the boat train arrived from London with its load of first and second class passengers. These went aboard the ship through the midships entrance on B deck, where they were met by stewards and shown to their cabins. First class passengers were

*Above:* Captain Smith and the deck officers of the *Titanic*. They are, rear row from left to right, Chief Purser Herbert McElroy, Second Officer Charles Herbert Lightoller, Third Officer Herbert Pitman, Fourth Officer Joseph Groves Boxhall, Fifth Officer Harold Godfrey Lowe; front row, Sixth Officer James Moody, Chief Officer Henry Tingle Wilde, Captain Edward John Smith and First Officer William McMaster Murdoch.

*Left:* First Officer Murdoch. Lost. *By kind permission of Philip Croucher of Rembrandt.*

given guide books to help them find their way around the ship. This turned out to be quite useful to many of the crew as they could always ask for directions from a guide book-flourishing passenger!

Individuals of all classes also made their own way to the ship, many first class from Southampton's elegant South Western Hotel. By the time the quayside was cleared, more than 900 passengers were exploring the vast interior of the new ship, but this was still less than a third of the number she was designed to carry.

Nevertheless the passengers aboard made up a fair representation of society from the very rich and famous in first class to the very poorest and most anonymous in steerage. By far the wealthiest man on the ship was Colonel John Jacob Astor, with an estimated fortune of around £30 million. The richest man aboard should have been John Pierpont Morgan, the line's owner, whose wealth and power probably exceeded that of any other man alive. Morgan had been booked to sail on *Titanic's* maiden voyage, along with a quantity of ancient Egyptian artefacts to be added to his New York collection.

*Above left:* Luigi Gatti's wife who came to see her husband off at Southampton. Many of the Italian restaurant staff aboard *Titanic* were employees of Gatti's famous London restaurant. With the single exception of Mr Gatti's secretary, Paul Mauge, all were lost.

*Above:* Second Wireless Operator Harold Sidney Bride, who survived.

*Left:* Senior Wireless Operator John (Jack) Phillips. Lost.

*Right:* The South Western Hotel at Southampton where many of *Titanic's* first class passengers stayed overnight before joining the ship on the morning of 10 April 1012.

However, Morgan had cancelled his booking at the last moment and had his artefacts removed from the ship's hold.

Isador Straus, an American politician and partner in Macy's department store, was another of the millionaires making the trip. Along for the ride were several other wealthy and influential Americans like Washington banker Clarence Moore, the war correspondent and artist Frank D. Millett, presidential advisor Major Archibald Willingham Butt and Charles Melville Hays, the president of the Grand Trunk railway. Not all of the rich and famous were Americans. William T. Stead, a noted English writer, editor and pacifist was on his way to America, at the personal invitation of President Taft, to address a meeting of the peace movement. War in Europe was looming and as the threat grew so did the peace movement that was trying to avert it. The President's advisor Archie Butt, had been in Europe as a personal messenger of the President's in an attempt to persuade the Pope to intercede in the growing hostility between Germany and her neighbours.

J. Bruce Ismay was making the voyage to check that the ship came up to expectation. In order to correct any minor defects Thomas Andrews and an eight man group of skilled workers from Harland & Wolff were sailing with the ship.

At about midday, with the assistance of several tugs, *Titanic* moved slowly away from the Southampton quayside. The most famous maiden voyage in history had begun, though all might still have been well were it not for the skill and vigilance of Captain Gale of the tug *Vulcan*.

As *Titanic* moved forward in the crowded dock the movement of water caused by her passage forced the SS *New York* to move away from the *Oceanic*, to which she was tied up. The thick mooring lines snapped with a sound like shots being fired, and *New York*'s stern began to swing towards *Titanic*. The liner's engines were put astern, which helped to slow *New York*'s swing but it was not enough on its own to prevent a collision. Captain Gale, on seeing what was happening, turned his tiny vessel away from the liner and hurried around to the far side of *New York*. At the second attempt Captain Gale managed to get a line on the rogue ship and arrest her swing towards *Titanic*. The incident delayed the departure of the White Star liner for about an hour.

*Titanic* dropped anchor off Cherbourg, 77 miles from Southampton, at about 6.30pm, still an hour behind schedule. The harbour was not big enough for the new liners to enter, so passengers and mail had to be ferried to and from the ship in tenders. First and second class passengers were conveyed aboard *Nomadic*, while third class were herded aboard her sister, *Traffic*. Waiting to board the liner at Cherbourg were 142 first — including Benjamin Guggenheim and his valet, Mrs J. (Margaret) Brown, better known as Molly and a Mr Morgan and his spouse who were really Sir Cosmo Duff Gordon and his wife, Lucile — 30 second and 102 third class passengers. At about 8.00pm the liner weighed anchor and got under way for Queenstown (now Cobh), near Cork, in Ireland. She arrived at about 11.30 the following morning.

It had already been noticed by some of the passengers, particularly

7149. South Western Hotel, Southampton.

T.S.S. "NEW YORK" LANDING U.S. MAILS
& PASSENGERS AT PLYMOUTH

*Top:* **The SS *New York* which almost prevented *Titanic's* maiden voyage from beginning on time when she broke her moorings and drifted into the path of the liner.**

*Above:* **The first class dining room on the *New York*.**

in second class, that the ship had a noticeable, and presumably incurable, list to port. When sitting in their dining saloon and looking out of the portholes on the starboard side they could see the sky; when looking out of the port side they could see only the sea.

Eight people left *Titanic* at Queenstown, seven of them passengers, and a deserter, John Coffy, who smuggled himself off the ship disguised as mail. Seven second and 113 third class passengers joined the ship, along with 1,385 sacks of mail, from the tenders *America* and *Ireland*.

As the vessel lay quietly at anchor Joseph Bruce Ismay, who normally refused to interfere in the day-to-day running of any White Star vessel, called for a meeting with the ship's Chief Engineer, Joseph Bell, and told him just what speed he expected the ship to make during the crossing, day by day. A high speed trial was also supposedly arranged for the following Monday morning to find out if *Titanic* was any faster than *Olympic*, which

had already been demonstrated during the short run from Belfast to Southampton. Incredibly, these arrangements were seemingly made without Captain Smith's knowledge or agreement.

Shortly after 1.30pm *Titanic* again weighed anchor, gave three deep blasts on her whistles, and moved slowly towards the Daunt lightship to drop off the pilot. It was just growing dusk on the evening of 11 April as the liner cleared the southern coast of Ireland and headed out into the North Atlantic, almost running down a small French fishing vessel in the process.

## Westwards

Instead of taking the 'Outward Southern Track' Captain Smith elected to take the shorter 'Autumn Southern Track', which took his ship about 60 miles further to the north.

The Arctic winter of 1911/12 had been milder than normal, and more icebergs than usual had found their way south into the North Atlantic. *Titanic's* route would take her to the north of some of them. During the ship's first full day at sea no fewer than five wireless warnings of icebergs either on, or close to, her intended route were received.

*Top: Neptune*, a Southampton harbour tug that assisted in manoeuvring *Titanic* and helped prevent a collision between the liner and the SS *New York*.

*Above: Titanic*, under the guiding influence of harbour tugs, making her way into the River Itchen, seen from the deck of another vessel.

*Above: Titanic* clearing the harbour entrance to her Southampton dock at the beginning of her maiden voyage. This view is from another vessel outside the harbour entrance.

*Left:* Chief Steward Andrew Latimer. Lost. *By kind permission of Philip Croucher of Rembrandt.*

*Right:* Purser R. L. Barker. Lost. *By kind permission of Philip Croucher of Rembrandt.*

On 12 April *Titanic* received more wireless ice warnings from *Avala, East Point, Manitou* and *Californian.* Responding to these early warnings *Titanic* increased speed to just over 21½kt. The ice was still more than 800 miles ahead of the speeding liner, but in order to be sure of reaching it before it went away *Titanic* increased speed yet again! From noon on Saturday to the same time on Sunday she averaged 22½kt. By Sunday morning 19 ice warnings had reached the ship.

Although clearly appreciating that they were approaching an area fraught with menace Captain Smith cancelled Sunday morning's lifeboat drill and held divine service instead. The captain had good reason for cancelling the boat drill, which would have made it clear to both passengers and crew that there were lifeboat places for only about half of them.

At 9.00am the first ice warning of the day arrived by wireless. It was from the SS *Caronia* and told of icebergs and growlers (icebergs that have partly melted and rolled over) almost directly ahead of the ship, seen two days before in position 42°N from 49°W to 51°W. Although this warning was delivered to the bridge, possibly the only one that day, it was ignored by the ship's officers.

Shortly after 1.30pm a further ice warning arrived, from the SS *Baltic*, another White Star liner. This warning told of large amounts of field ice dead ahead of *Titanic*. Captain Smith acknowledged the warning, so we know that it reached him, but the bridge officers were unaware of its existence. Certainly the ship's navigating officer, Boxhall, never saw it. Instead of taking this message to the bridge, Captain Smith handed it to J. Bruce Ismay, who, after glancing at it, put it in his pocket, where it remained until about 7.15 that evening.

Only three minutes after the warning from *Baltic* had been received another message arrived, this one from the German steamer *Amerika*. The *Amerika's* warning was of icebergs, also dead ahead of the liner.

When these last two warnings were received *Titanic* was heading S62°W, just a little to the west of southwest. At 5.15pm the liner was due to change course on to a heading of S86°W, nearly due west. Almost as if he wanted to be sure that he didn't miss the ice field ahead of his vessel Captain Smith delayed the turn to the west for half an hour, putting the ship a few miles to the south of where it otherwise would have been. On her new course the White Star

liner would pass within a couple of miles of the ice reported by *Baltic* at about 10.30 that evening.

At 7.30pm another warning was received. This particular message was not even intended for the *Titanic* but had been sent to the Leyland Line's *Antillian* from the same company's *Californian*. The *Californian* had encountered icebergs at about 6.30pm (ship's time), about five miles to the south of 42°5'N, 49°9'W. Having transmitted his warning Captain Lord hastened on westwards until he, at about 10.15, came across a large field of ice, when his sense of urgency evaporated and *Californian* stopped for the night. Captain Lord calculated his position as 42°5'N, 50°7'W.

Second wireless operator Harold Bride, who received the *Californian* ice warning, chose to impale it on a metal spike instead of taking it straight to the bridge. He later claimed that he handed the warning to an officer on the bridge, although he could not recall which officer it was; but then Bride later claimed a lot of things that are demonstrably untrue.

Contrary to company orders, which required the master to be on the bridge in all but ideal conditions, Captain Smith was attending a private dinner party given in the first class à la carte restaurant in his honour. He did not leave the restaurant until five minutes to nine that evening.

Showing some appreciation of the danger facing the ship even before the *Californian's* warning was received, First Officer Murdoch ordered Lamp Trimmer Samuel Hemmings to ensure that there were no lights visible forward of the bridge that might interfere with the lookouts' view. He was also keeping an eye on both air and water temperature. By 9.00pm the air temperature had fallen to 33°F (1°C) and Murdoch worried that there were icebergs close by.

At 8.00pm Archie Jewell and George Symons took over as lookouts from George Hogg and Frank Evans. Symons was well aware that on such a moonless night his ears and nose would be as much use to him as his eyes. He sniffed the air and immediately picked up a faint but unmistakable odour: icebergs. Down on the deck, without being entirely sure of what it was, first class passenger Miss Elizabeth Shutes had also detected the aroma.

Captain Smith made his way to the bridge at about 9.00pm and engaged Second Officer Charles Lightoller, who was on duty, in conversation about the unusually fine weather. Smith said, 'There is not much wind,' to which Lightoller replied, 'No, it is a flat calm.' 'A flat calm.' Smith repeated. 'Quite flat; there is no wind.'

After about 25 minutes on the bridge Captain Smith decided to turn in for the night. Before leaving, he left instructions that he was to be called immediately if things became 'at all doubtful'. Lightoller was undismayed; he was certain that from his position on the bridge he would be able to spot any iceberg before the ship came within a couple of miles of it. Unfortunately Mr Lightoller would not be on the bridge after 10.00pm.

Not long after Captain Smith retired for the night Lightoller ordered Sixth Officer Moody to instruct the lookouts to keep a sharp lookout for ice. Moody was to impress on them the necessity of passing the instructions on to whoever took over their duties in the crow's nest at 10.00pm.

*Right:* An aerial view of Southampton Docks much as they would have appeared in 1912. *Olympic* is moored at the White Star berth in the Ocean Dock, top right.

*Below:* White Star Line's Southampton Offices in Canute Road as they appeared in the late 1990s.

At 9.40pm yet another ice warning was received by Phillips, in the wireless room. 'From *Mesaba* to *Titanic*. In latitude 43°N to 41°25'N, longitude 49° to long 50°30'W. Saw much heavy pack ice and great numbers large icebergs, also field ice. Weather good, clear.' *Mesaba's* wireless operator, Stanley Howard Adams, received an acknowledgement, 'Received, thanks,' but he was convinced that this came from Phillips, and not any of *Titanic's* senior officers. He was right. The warning never got any further than *Titanic's* wireless room. During the day, equipment problems had allowed a backlog of passenger's personal messages to accumulate and the operators were preoccupied with these. They completely ignored the directive that messages relating to the safe navigation of the ship should take unconditional precedence over all others.

The watch changed at 10.00pm. Lightoller handed over to First Officer Murdoch, but Sixth Officer Moody remained on the bridge. Quartermaster Robert Hitchens took over the ship's wheel from fellow Quartermaster Alfred Olliver. Like Moody, Olliver remained on duty as a standby helmsman. During the changeover on the bridge Lightoller should have passed on Captain Smith's instructions to call him at once if things became 'at all doubtful', but he failed to do so.

Up in the crow's nest lookouts Fred Fleet and Reginald Lee relieved Jewel and Symons. Unlike the Second Officer, Jewel and Symons did pass on their instructions to keep a special lookout for ice. Lee, like Symons earlier, sniffed the air, and smelled icebergs.

About half an hour after Murdoch had taken over on the liner's bridge another vessel was sighted to starboard. The *Rappahannock*, travelling in the opposite direction to *Titanic*, signalled by Morse lamp that she had just passed through a large icefield and had seen many icebergs. The ice, which now lay directly ahead of the White Star liner, had damaged the *Rappahannock's* steering gear. The Morse lamp on *Titanic's* bridge flashed a reply, 'Message received. Thank you. Good night.' Things had, without question, become 'doubtful'.

At 22½kt *Titanic* charged blindly on, towards the ice that now lay only about 25 miles ahead.

Aboard *Californian* Captain Lord ordered his wireless operator, Evans, to contact *Titanic* and pass on both his position and that of the ice to their south. At 10.55pm Evans began to transmit, not knowing just how close to them *Titanic* really was.

Phillips was still busily transmitting passengers' personal messages when the incoming signal from *Californian* cut across everything. It was so loud that Phillips had to snatch the earphones from his head. Without allowing Evans time to complete his message Phillips angrily sent, 'Keep out. Shut up. You're jamming my signal. I'm working Cape Race.' Evans gave up, and instead sat and listened to *Titanic* working with Cape Race before finally switching off his wireless and preparing for bed, at about 11.30pm.

Somewhere relatively close by, the Royal Navy's Second Class Cruiser HMS *Sirius*, patrolling off Newfoundland, must have overheard *Californian's* and *Titanic's* signals. She maintained radio silence, as she would throughout the whole incident.

**Second Electrician Alfred Samuel Allsop. Lost.** *By kind permission of Philip Croucher of Rembrandt.*

Outside warnings of the proximity of ice had reached *Titanic*, and had been totally ignored. Now it was up to the lookouts in the crow's nest and the officers on the bridge. Disregarding warnings from her own lookouts should have been beyond the pale even for the officers of the *Titanic*, but it wasn't.

In the crow's nest, Fred Fleet and Reginald Lee peered into the darkness ahead and to the sides of the ship. Fleet described the conditions: 'It was the beautiful-est night I ever seen. The stars were like lamps.' Sometime shortly after 11.00pm the lookouts noticed a patch of haze directly ahead of the ship, extending about three points (33¾°) either side of the bow. Fleet reached across and grabbed the rope hanging from the crow's nest bell, ringing it three times; the recognised signal to the bridge that there was an obstruction dead ahead. The time was 11.15pm.

Fleet had seen 'A black object, high above the water, right ahead.' Next he picked up the telephone that should have connected him to the bridge. The telephone rang but there was no answer, giving Fleet the impression that there was nobody on the bridge. The ship raced onwards, straight towards the 'bluish'

*Above:* Steward Frank Allsop of Obelisk Road, Southampton. Lost. *By kind permission of Philip Croucher of Rembrandt.*

*Above right:* Two survivors from *Titanic*. On the left is Able Seaman Thomas Jones who made his escape aboard Boat 8, which left the sinking ship less than half full because, according to Jones, there were not enough women and children on the boat deck to fill it. On the right is Quartermaster George Rowe who saw lifeboats in the water within a couple of minutes of the collision, a full hour before the first of *Titanic's* boats was lowered. *By kind permission of Philip Croucher of Rembrandt.*

coloured iceberg silhouetted against the star-spangled sky, about 11 miles away from the ship.

Two or three times more Fleet rang the bell and tried the telephone before he finally got a reply. He was not sure of exactly who he spoke to, but whoever it was took no action to avoid the iceberg.

Fireman John (Jack) Podesta while lying in bed talking to a mate heard Fleet's cry of 'Ice ahead, sir' several times. The fireman also noted that the warnings produced no reaction from those controlling the ship.

The lack of action from the bridge alarmed the lookouts as they knew the ship was on a collision course with the iceberg. Fleet realised that if the ship struck head-on then the foremast, complete with crow's nest and lookouts, would almost certainly break off and go overboard. Being the senior of the two he ordered Lee down from the crow's nest to report in person, to the bridge, the iceberg ahead of the ship. After all, there was no point in them both going overboard with the mast. Lee started to obey Fleet's orders, knowing full well why they had been issued. He got as far as the bottom of the mast before loyalty to Fleet drove him back up to the crow's nest. In the time he had been away Fred Fleet had tried yet again to contact the bridge, first by ringing the bell three times and then trying the telephone. This time Sixth Officer Moody answered, 'Yes. What did you see?'

'Iceberg right ahead,' said Fleet, for the umpteenth time.

'Thank you,' replied Moody before ringing off.

Even as he was talking to Moody, Fleet noticed *Titanic's* bow beginning to swing to port, indicating that the iceberg had been seen from the bridge before his last alarm call had been received. There would inevitably be a small delay between the ship's rudder being put hard over and the vessel starting to respond. *Titanic* needed about half a mile to turn 90° to either starboard or port, at 20kt. At more than 22kt she would need even more room; room that was no longer available. The two lookouts, who had first tried to warn the ship's officers of the presence of the iceberg when it was more than 10 miles from the liner, stood rooted to their stations in the crow's nest.

*Left:* **Alexander James Littlejohn, a steward on the** *Titanic,* **as he appeared in January 1911 (left) and after surviving the sinking (right).**

*Right:* **William T. Stead, a famous English writer and editor of the** *Pall Mall Gazette,* **who was on his way to America at the personal invitation of President Taft.**

On the bridge Murdoch had seen the iceberg at about the same moment as Fred Fleet had rung the alarm bell for the last time. Instinctively he had ordered the engines put 'full-astern' and the helm to 'hard-a-starboard'. (Helm orders of the period, left over from the days when ships were steered with a tiller, meant exactly the reverse of what they appeared. 'Hard-a-starboard' [starboard = right] was therefore the order for an emergency turn to port/left.) Quartermaster Hitchens spun the wheel for all he was worth.

Up in the crow's nest Fleet and Lee watched as *Titanic's* bow slowly swung clear of the iceberg. Then, as the foremast came abreast of the berg, Fleet noticed a slight grinding noise that lasted about 10 seconds. There was no noticeable impact as far as the lookouts were concerned. As Fred Fleet said later, 'I thought it was a narrow shave.' Relieved, Fleet and Lee settled down to complete their spell in the crow's nest.

Captain Smith emerged from his cabin on to the bridge about three or four minutes after the 'narrow shave'. 'What is it?' asked the Captain. 'An iceberg,' Murdoch replied. Without further ado Captain Smith ordered the watertight doors closed throughout the ship, only to be informed by First Officer Murdoch that this had already been done.

First Officer Murdoch explained to the Captain what had occurred and what steps he had taken to prevent, or minimise, the accident. 'I was going to port around it, but there was no time,' he told Smith. Murdoch meant by 'port around' that once the ship's bow had swung clear of the obstruction the helm would be reversed to push the stern clear as well. The helmsman, Quartermaster Robert Hitchens, later confirmed that the ship had never been under a port helm (starboard rudder) either before or after the collision; and if anybody was in a position to know, it was Hitchens. As she slowed, *Titanic's* bow continued to swing southwards, away from the *Californian* lying stopped just a few miles below the horizon.

Smith sent for the carpenter and ordered him to sound the ship before checking the wheelhouse instruments, only to discover that *Titanic* had a 5° list to starboard. Until then the ship had listed incurably to port.

The liner had almost come to a stop when the standby helmsman, Quartermaster Alfred Olliver, noted that the Captain ordered the engines half ahead. Before Olliver could take in much more he was ordered to take messages to various parts of the ship not connected to the bridge by the telephone system. This left just the helmsman, Robert Hitchens, to witness what else happened on the bridge, at least for a while.

*Left:* *Titanic* in Southampton Water.

*Above:* *Olympic* posses as her sister with *Titanic's* name on the bow in oversize letters.

128 CHERBOURG. — *Vue sur le port et la digue.* — ND. Phot.

*Left:* Cherbourg, as it was when visited by *Titanic* in 1912. The liner was too big to enter the harbour and was obliged to anchor outside.

*Below: Titanic's* second port of call was Queenstown (now Cobh), close to Cork, in southern Ireland.

*Right:* Queenstown as it appeared in 1912.

*Below right:* On her arrival at Queenstown *Titanic* would have anchored off Roche's Point.

GREETINGS FROM QUEENSTOWN CO.CORK.

ST. COLMAN'S CATHEDRAL, QUEENSTOWN, CO. CORK.

VIEW FROM THE BEACH, QUEENSTOWN.

QUEENSTOWN. CO. CORK.

WEST BEACH, QUEENSTOWN.

QUEENSTOWN FROM THE CHURCH TOWER.

QUEENSTOWN HARBOUR

*Le Paquebot géant " Olympic " en rade de Cherbourg*
*Longueur 268 mètres ; largeur 29 mètres ; hauteur du Pont supérieur au dessus de l'eau, 27 mètres ·*

Collection F. C., Cherbourg

CHERBOURG - Le " TRAFFIC " bateau transbordeur de la " White star Line "
quitte la gare Maritime

*Above: Olympic* at
Cherbourg with the
tender *Traffic* alongside.

*Left:* The White Star
third class tender *Traffic*,
which carried 102 third
class passengers out to
*Titanic* at Cherbourg.
*By kind permission of
Philip Croucher of
Rembrandt.*

Embarking Passengers, Queenstown

RMS "TITANIC" TENDERS
'AMERICA' AND 'IRELAND'
QUEENSTOWN 1912

*Above:* The tenders *Ireland* and *America* brought 120 passengers and 1,385 sacks of mail out to *Titanic* at Queenstown, and took off eight people that wanted to leave. Seven of those leaving the ship were legitimate passengers, but the eighth was Fireman John Coffy who was deserting for reasons of his own. As at Cherbourg, *Titanic* was too big to enter the harbour.

*Left:* Amongst those passengers leaving *Titanic* at Queenstown were Jack Odell and his family. *By kind permission of Philip Croucher of Rembrandt.*

*Above, below and right:* The last clear views *Titanic's* passengers would have had of Queenstown as they left for their various destinations, some unplanned.

*Below right:* Passengers on the promenade deck of a White Star liner.

Queenstown from the Water

*Above:* The tender *Ireland* at the Queenstown quayside where *Titanic* passengers would have embarked.

*Left:* The tender *America* alongside *Titanic. By kind permission of Philip Croucher of Rembrandt.*

*Above right:* First class passengers aboard *Titanic* at Queenstown, looking forward to their voyage.

*Right:* The organ specially commissioned for *Titanic*. The builder of this organ was taken ill with believed influenza and was unable to deliver the organ on time. As he was supposed to sail with the ship on her maiden voyage, to sort out any problems that might crop up, this is a very rare example of influenza probably saving someone's life.

*Far right:* A replica of one of *Titanic's* 159 boiler furnaces.

# TWO HEROES IN "WIRELESS" ROOM.

## How Junior Fixed Lifebelt Round Comrade Who Went on Working.

A wonderfully moving story is told by Mr. Harold Bride, the junior Marconi operator on the Titanic.

It was dictated in the wireless room of the Carpathia, where, though injured, he had bravely kept working until port was reached.

After describing how the wireless call for help sent by Phillips had been answered by the Carpathia, and he went to Captain Smith and informed him of it, he continues:—

"I came back and heard Phillips giving the Carpathia fuller directions.

"I noticed that the list forward was increasing. Phillips told me that the wireless was growing weaker.

"I went out on deck and looked around. The water was close up to the boat deck. There was a great scramble aft, and how poor Phillips worked through it I don't know.

"He was a brave man. I learned to love him that night, for I suddenly felt for him a great reverence, seeing him standing there sticking to his work while everybody else was raging about. I will never forget the work of Phillips in the last awful fifteen minutes.

### CAPTAIN'S LAST WORDS.

"I thought it was about time to look about to see if there was anything detached that would float. I remembered that my special lifebelt was under the bunk and went and got it.

"I saw Phillips standing out there still sending away, giving the Carpathia details just how we were doing.

"We picked up the Olympic and told her we were sinking by the head.

"'We're ..bout all down.' As Phillips was sending that message I strapped his lifebelt to his back. I had already put on his overcoat and his boots. He suggested if I could get him into his boots or if any with a sort of laugh that I should look out and see if all the people were off in the boats or if any boats were left, or how things were.

"I saw a collapsible boat near the funnel, and went over to it. Twelve men were trying to boost it down to the boat deck. They were having an awful time. It was the last boat left.

"I walked back to Phillips and said: 'The last raft is gone.' Then came the captain's voice:

Men, you have done your full duty. You can do no more. Abandon your cabin now. It's every man for himself. You look out for yourselves. I release you—that's the way of it 'at this kind of time, every man for himself.'

"I looked out. The boat deck was awash. Phillips clung on—sending—sending. He clung on for about ten minutes, or maybe fifteen minutes, after the captain released him. The water was then coming into our cabin while he worked.

### FIGHT IN THE CABIN.

"Something happened now that I hate to tell about. I was back in my room getting Phillips' money for him. As I looked out of the door I saw a stoker or somebody from below decks leaning over Phillips from behind. Phillips was too busy to notice what the man was doing. He was slipping the lifebelt off Phillips' back.

"He was a big man, too, and as you can see I am very small. I don't know what it was I got hold of. I remembered in a flash the way Phillips had clung on; how I had to fix that lifebelt in place because he was too busy to do it.

"I knew that the man from below decks had his own lifebelt and should have known where to get it. I suddenly felt a passion not to let that man die a decent sailor's death. I wished he might have stretched a rope or walked the plank. I did my duty. I hope I finished him; I don't know. We left him on the cabin floor of the wireless room, and he wasn't moving.

"Phillips ran aft, and that was the last I saw of him. I went to the place where I had seen a collapsible boat on the boat deck. A large wave came awash of the deck and carried the boat off.

"I had hold of an oarlock. I went off with it, and the next I knew I was in the boat, and the boat was upside down, I under it.

"I remember realising that whatever happened I must breathe. I knew I had to fight for it, and did. How I got out from under the boat I don't know, but I felt a breath of air at last.

"I swam with all my might. I was sinking. I was very cold. I saw a boat of some kind near me, and put all my strength into the effort to swim to it.

"It was hard work, and I was all but done when a hand reached out from the boat and pulled me aboard. It was our same collapsible boat.

"There was just room for me to roll on the edge, and I lay there, not caring what happened. Somebody sat on my legs, causing me pain, and I hadn't the heart left to ask the man to move.

"It was a terrible sight. All around men were swimming and sinking. I lay where I was, letting the man wrench my feet out of shape. Others came near, but nobody gave them a hand.

"At last the Carpathia was alongside, and the people were being taken up by a rope ladder. Our boat drew near, and one by one the men were taken off.

"One man was dead. I passed him. He was Phillips. He had died on a raft from exposure and cold.

"He had been 'all in' from work before the wreck came. He stood his ground until the crisis had passed and then had collapsed, I suppose."

*Left:* One of Second Wireless Operator Bride's several versions of events aboard *Titanic*, and his own escape, as reported in the *Daily Mirror*, 20 April 1912. On the evidence of this newspaper report, had it been true, could Bride have been charged with attempted murder or manslaughter?

*Right:* The wireless room of a 1912 liner. *By kind permission of Philip Croucher of Rembrandt.*

THE WRECK OF THE TITANIC

*Right:* A contemporary artist's impression of *Titanic's* encounter with an iceberg.

*Below:* A Dutch card showing *Titanic* battling her way through heavy seas. In reality the ship never encountered anything rougher than a gentle Atlantic swell. *By kind permission of Philip Croucher of Rembrandt.*

Titanic vergaan op 15 April 1912.

„NEARER MY GOD TO THEE"

Nader, mijn God bij
Zij ook de weg daa
Wat ook mijn toekomst
Nader mijn God, bij

*Above: Titanic's* engineers who kept the lights burning and the pumps running right to the end. The little evidence that exists suggests that not a single engineer deserted his post during the sinking. All were lost.

*Left:* Junior Assistant Second Engineer Jonathan Shepherd who broke a leg when the boiler room lights failed for a few moments immediately after the collision. Although unable to move, Shepherd and another junior assistant second engineer, Herbert Harvey, managed to get the pumps started in Boiler Room 5, more than half an hour before Captain Smith gave orders to do so, and for a short time appeared to have the situation under control. When the bulkhead at the forward end of Boiler Room 5 collapsed and the sea rushed in, Harvey was last seen going to the aid of his disabled colleague.

# AMONG THE ICE

The shock of collision was so slight that most people aboard *Titanic* hardly noticed it. Nevertheless it had presumably opened a series of wounds over about a third of the ship's length. Marine architect, Edward Wilding, a member of *Titanic's* design team, later described the likely extent of the damage as equivalent to a 200ft-long, $^1/_2$in-wide split in the hull with a total area of only about 12sq ft.

One immediately noticeable effect of the collision was a considerable amount of ice that supposedly fell from the berg on to the forward well deck. The iceberg, according to first class passenger Colonel Archibald Gracie, towered 50ft above A deck and must, for ice to have fallen on to *Titanic's* deck, have overhung it. Why then didn't the starboard bridge wing, which projected out from the rest of the superstructure, and Boat 1, which was always kept swung out, come into contact with this overhanging iceberg?

Photographs taken on the morning of 15 April 1912 show a berg with red paint scrapings along its waterline, generally believed to be the one the ship struck. But if it was then the ice on the well deck came from somewhere else. The iceberg in the photographs is shaped much like the Rock of Gibraltar and could not have overhung *Titanic's* decks. The most likely place for the ice to have come from is the ship's own rigging and wireless antenna.

In the wireless room senior operator Jack Phillips noticed a slight jolt and the ship's engines stopping, while second operator, Harold Bride, slept through the incident undisturbed.

Right at the stern of the ship Quartermaster George Thomas Rowe was checking the Cherub Patent Log when he noticed a very slight jar at the moment of impact, and he saw an iceberg pass very close to the starboard side of *Titanic's* stern. He also noticed that there were two lifeboats in the water, off the liner's starboard quarter, no more than 25 seconds after the bump. The only way, if those boats came from *Titanic*, that they could have been in the water then is if they were knocked off the ship during the collision. No witnesses reported boats being lost this way.

Shortly after the collision Colonel Gracie made a tour of the boat deck and found nothing amiss: William Stead and Father Byles had been on deck throughout the incident and did not think anything of note had happened. Neither did a middle aged couple strolling arm in arm around the second class promenade deck. Perhaps Rowe's lifeboats came from another ship!

In the first class smoking room Hugh Woolner noticed '. . . a sort of stopping, a sort of — not exactly shock, but a sort of slowing down'. Some people hurried outside hoping to see an iceberg, Woolner concluded. He, Spencer V. Silverthorne and a steward were the only ones in the room to see a berg as it passed alongside; nobody else saw anything.

Steward Alfred Crawford, who was on duty at the forward end of B deck, noticed a slight 'crunch' on the starboard side. He looked out of a porthole and saw 'a large black object', reaching much higher than B deck, passing close alongside. Passengers in the second class smoking room tried to estimate the size of the iceberg, finally settling on a height of about 80–90ft.

In the mess at the forward port side of C deck, Seamen Buley, Osman and Brice were sitting down and talking when they heard the crow's nest bell ring three times. Seconds later Buley felt a 'slight jar. It seemed as though something was rubbing alongside of her at the time.' Brice thought it felt more 'like a heavy vibration'. (The ship's engines being suddenly put full-astern from full-ahead would have caused just the sort of vibration Brice described.)

On the other side of the ship, much closer to the point of impact, Fireman Jack Podesta noticed nothing more than a noise 'like tearing calico'. Mrs E. D. Appleton, a first class passenger, described the noise of the collision in exactly the same words as Podesta. Able Seaman Joseph Scarrott thought he felt the ship's engines going astern, about eight minutes after the warning bell was sounded in the crow's nest, and that the ship had not struck anything at all.

Mr and Mrs Walter Douglas were in their stateroom, C86, when the ship struck. 'The shock of the collision was not great,' they said.

Mrs J. Stuart White described it as '. . . just as though we went over a thousand marbles. There was nothing terrifying about it at all.' Other passengers were equally unimpressed by the violence of the crash. Major Arthur Peuchen thought it like a large wave striking the ship. Mrs Walter B. Stephenson likened it 'to the first shock of the San Francisco earthquake'. And Marguerite Frolicher described it as, 'Like the Zurich lake ferry making a sloppy landing.' C. H. Stengel, who had just been woken by his wife, heard a slight crash to which he paid no attention.

The firemen, quartered in the bows down on D deck felt the impact more keenly. John Thompson 'felt the crash with all its force up there in the eyes of the ship'. According to him, he and his mates were thrown from their bunks. Shortly afterwards Leading Fireman William Small rushed in and ordered, 'All hands below!' The firemen were unable to obey the order because their tunnel beneath the forward holds was rapidly filling with water. This tunnel, considered by the designers to be so vital to the safety of the ship, that it had its own pumps and watertight doors, at no point came closer to the outer hull of the ship than 63in. The ice, if there really was any ice, had penetrated at least that far. On seeing the flooded tunnel the leading fireman ordered the rest to find their lifejackets and make their way to the boat deck.

Further aft on D deck, in the dining saloon, stewards felt only a slight grinding jar. James Johnson believed it was nothing more than the liner dropping a propeller blade, a belief shared by Joseph Thomas Wheat and millionaire passenger Howard Case.

At the forward end of E deck were the trimmers' quarters. The impact was less noticeable here than on the deck above. Immediately after the collision Lamp Trimmer Samuel Hemmings, who was in his bunk, noticed a peculiar hissing sound caused by air being forced out of the top of the forepeak tank as it filled with seawater from below. The hull was breached as far forward as possible.

On the starboard side, in cabin E50, Mr and Mrs George A. Harder felt nothing more than a little vibration, and heard a scraping noise. James R. McGough had a similar experience except that splinters of ice came into his cabin, through the open porthole. Further aft on the port side, in the stewards' quarters, Frederick Dent Ray noticed nothing more than 'a kind of movement that went backward and forward'. He thought something had gone wrong in the engine room or a propeller had failed.

Dent Ray lay in bed for another quarter of an hour before he heard the order to close the watertight doors on E deck. By that time the two corridors running fore and aft, known as 'Park Lane' and 'Scotland Road', were full of third class passengers and crewmen all trying to make their way aft. The watertight doors in the corridors were closed, effectively sealing in those passengers who remained in the forward third class part of the ship, to be drowned like rats in a trap.

Stewards Samuel J. Rule and John Edward Hart slept through the incident, undisturbed. Another steward, William Ward, noticed the collision and went so far as to get out of bed, open the porthole in order to take a look outside, and decide that there was nothing amiss. First class passenger Norman Campbell Chambers heard

what he thought were 'jangling chains whipping along the sides of the ship'. The noise passed so quickly that he put it down to some sort of failure of the starboard engine.

Down on G deck, the lowest deck in the ship with passenger accommodation, again the shock of collision was extraordinarily slight. Fireman Charles Hendricksen slept through it, only to be wakened a few moments later by a crewmate and the sound of seawater swirling round the foot of the spiral staircase connecting the firemen's quarters to the passageway beneath the forward holds. In the forward open dormitory berths third class passenger Olaus Abelseth was woken by the noise of the impact. One of the other passengers there, Daniel Buckley, noticed that water was already beginning to creep into their quarters.

On the tank top, the very lowest deck in the ship, were the boiler and engine rooms. Fireman Fred Barrett had been working in Boiler Room 6 and had just stopped for a chat with Second Engineer James Hesketh when the warning bell sounded and a red light came on. Moments later came a crash, and a jet of water burst through the side of the ship, for the full length of the boiler room, about 2ft above the floor. Not waiting for further instructions Barrett and Hesketh fled aft to Number 5. The watertight door between the boiler rooms closed behind them. Barrett clambered up the escape ladder from Number 5 and peered down into the boiler room they had just vacated. There was already 8ft of water in there.

The boiler room lights had gone out and Barrett was sent to fetch lamps. On his return he and some other firemen checked the boilers, only to find that they were dangerously low on water. He ran to the engineers and told them, and was promptly ordered to get more firemen down to draw the fires, before the boilers exploded.

For a while the forward bunker in Number 5 boiler room, which was also open to the sea, managed to contain the water that poured through the ship's side. The bunker had never been designed to hold water and ultimately failed, collapsing under the weight of seawater within. Barrett 'saw a wave of green foam come tearing through the boilers'. The fireman jumped for the escape ladder and scurried up, out of harm's way. The engineers were not so fortunate.

The collision, if that is what it was, as described by the witnesses seems to be a fairly minor event. Nobody describes the ship's course being abruptly changed as it must have been if the liner was shouldered aside by the much heavier iceberg. Nobody describes the ship's heavy bow framing being torn apart, as it must have been for the iceberg to have reached and punctured the 'firemen's passageway'. Nobody describes the entire ship being bodily thrown 20ft sideways as it must have been if the calculations of the United States Hydrographic Office are to be believed. For the benefit of the American Senate Inquiry into the loss of the *Titanic*, the Hydrographic Office worked out what sort of blow would be needed for an iceberg to inflict the damage and to cause the vessel to founder in the manner described by survivors. The force of the blow with which the liner struck the iceberg would have to be about 1,173,200ft tons, they calculated. This is approximately equal to

Titanic being struck by a full broadside from a contemporary battleship. In other words, the impact described by survivors and the damage to, and consequent foundering of, the liner are incompatible with the ship striking an iceberg.

## Calling for Help

Fourth Officer Boxhall, on his way to the bridge, heard the warning bells immediately preceding the collision and Murdoch's order 'hard-a-starboard'. On his arrival he noticed that the engine room telegraph was at full-astern. Shortly afterwards Captain Smith ordered him to go and check on the damage.

During his quick tour of inspection Boxhall was told by a postal clerk, John Jago Smith, that water was pouring into the mail room and decided he had better tell the captain straight away. On his way back to the bridge he roused Second Officer Lightoller and Third Officer Pitman. Neither officer had realised there was anything amiss. Boxhall reached the bridge at about 11.55pm and reported to Smith. He was closely followed by Lightoller and Pitman. Ten minutes later Captain Smith ordered Murdoch, with Lightoller's assistance, to begin uncovering the lifeboats and swinging them out.

While this was happening, J. Bruce Ismay arrived on the bridge and asked the captain if the ship was seriously damaged. He was told that the forepeak and forward four compartments were open to the sea, and that the ship was sinking.

Fred Fleet and Reginald Lee were relieved in the crow's nest at midnight by lookouts Hogg and Evans. For the next 25 minutes Hogg and Evans repeatedly tried to contact the bridge by telephone, without success. Then, at about 12.30am, without ever establishing contact with the bridge, they gave up and deserted the crow's nest.

Boxhall, who was a specialist in navigation, was ordered by the captain to work out Titanic's position. It took him a few minutes to calculate that the ship was at 41°46'N, 50°14'W. He wrote the position on a scrap of paper and took it to the Captain. In the meantime Captain Smith had estimated the ship's position himself as about 41°46'N, 50°23'W or 41°44'N, 50°24'W and had ordered Phillips to transmit a distress call with the estimated positions included. At 12.15am La Provence received a distress call giving the first position. Captain Smith took Boxhall's calculated position to the wireless room himself and a distress call was transmitted, and at 12.18am Ypiranga and Mount Temple both received a distress call giving the second position. The corrected signal was received at 12.25am by wireless operator Harold Cottam aboard the Cunard liner Carpathia and thus began one of the most bizarre rescues in history.

Cottam, after checking that the distress call was genuine, hurried to the bridge to raise the alarm. Carpathia's captain, Arthur Henry Rostron, had turned in for the night and the First Mate, H. V. Dean, was on duty. At first Dean did not believe the wireless operator but Cottam managed to persuade him that he was serious. Marching the wireless operator before him, Dean hurried to the captain's cabin and burst in. The captain, who was in bed but not asleep, was understandably annoyed at the intrusion and angrily demanded an explanation for this invasion of his privacy. Cottam quickly explained, 'Sir, I have just received an urgent distress call from Titanic. She requires immediate assistance. She has struck an iceberg and is sinking. Her position is 41°46'N, 50°14'W.' Even as Cottam spoke, Captain Rostron was getting out of bed and reaching for his clothes.

Minutes later Captain Rostron was in his chartroom working out the precise position of Titanic in relation to his own vessel. The ships were 58 miles apart when Rostron issued orders that Carpathia's course was to be changed to N52°W. Rostron issued orders that all of the ship's lifeboats should be swung out ready for instant use. His own passengers were to be told that the ship was going to the assistance of another vessel and should remain in their cabins, out of the way. He next sent for Chief Engineer Johnson and instructed him to rouse all of the extra firemen he needed to squeeze every possible scrap of speed out of Carpathia. Then, so as not to fritter away any of the extra heat generated by the stokers' efforts, the captain ordered the heating and hot water supplies to passenger and crew accommodation alike shut down. Johnson and his crew performed a minor miracle. Normally Carpathia's top speed was no more than 14kt but with the whole ship shaking to the pounding of her engines she raced towards Titanic at 17½kt. Knowing that Titanic had already struck an iceberg, and that the same fate might befall his own ship, Captain Rostron ordered a dozen extra lookouts in the crow's nest, bridge wings and in the bows of the ship.

Nineteen and a half miles away from Titanic, to the north, Cyril Evans, Californian's wireless operator, slept. Not that it made a scrap of difference to what was about to happen as the space between the ships was choked with ice and not navigable at night. But up on the bridge Captain Lord was watching a steamer approaching them from the southeast and showing just a masthead and a deck light. Lord estimated the mystery ship to be about the same size as Californian and about five miles away. Californian signalled with her Morse lamp, but the stranger made no reply. Captain Lord noticed that the unidentified vessel had stopped and extinguished her deck lights at 11.30pm but she got under way and moved off towards the southwest about 2½ hours later, although by then Captain Lord had turned in for the night. During the time they were watching this mysterious vessel Californian's officers saw five white rockets, or more likely roman candles, fired. As these 'rockets' did not reach anything like the height proper distress rockets should have done Californian's officers decided that they were nothing more than company signals, used by ships not equipped with wireless to communicate at night instead of employing a Morse lamp. As they believed there was no cause for alarm the officers did not disturb Captain Lord until after the mystery ship had left. When he was informed, Lord was only interested in discovering if there were any coloured rockets seen, but all were white. It seems that Captain Lord was expecting to see coloured rockets fired sometime during that night.

Aboard Titanic Thomas Andrews explained to Captain Smith that as the ship had taken on about 16,000 tons of water during the first 40 minutes after the collision it was only a matter of time before the ship's bows sank low enough to allow the water to pour over the tops of the forward bulkheads. Only then, almost 45 minutes after the collision, did Captain Smith order the ship's pumps started. It was too late; most of the pumps in the affected areas of the ship were already under water and no longer accessible.

Andrews could have mentioned that if the watertight doors throughout the ship were opened then the vessel would tend to go down on an even keel. As it would take considerably longer for water to fill the entire ship than just the five forward compartments she would have remained afloat for longer, and more of the pumps could have been brought into play. Everything forward that could have been jettisoned should have been, like the forward anchors and chains. Sails, which all ships of the time carried, could have been dropped over the starboard bow where water entering the ship would have dragged them into the punctures in the hull. Aft compartments could have been flooded to help balance the extra weight in the bows and hold them up. This is known as 'counter flooding' and is a recognised means of damage control on warships. On *Titanic* nothing was done. It was almost as if Captain Smith did not want to keep his ship afloat.

At about 12.25am, the order was given to begin loading the lifeboats. Already panic had broken out aboard.

## Abandon Ship

Second Officer Lightoller elected to load and lower Boat 4 first. The boat was lowered to A deck and first class passengers were instructed to go down from the boat deck and get into it. However, the forward end of A deck, where the boat waited, was enclosed with glass windows and nobody knew how to open them. To make matters worse, the ship's sounding spar projected from the hull directly below Boat 4. It took more than an hour to open the windows and to chop away the sounding spar.

At about the same time as Lightoller ordered Boat 4 down to A deck, Fourth Officer Boxhall was given permission to start firing distress rockets. *Titanic's* distress rockets were not rockets at all but mortar shells fired from a special socket on the bridge, which reached a height in excess of 800ft before bursting with a terrific bang and releasing a shower of red, white or blue stars. Quartermaster Olliver was despatched to the poop deck to collect the mortar bombs and Quartermaster Rowe, who was still on duty there. Rowe and Olliver each brought a box of 12 signals to the bridge, and Boxhall began firing them skywards. The signals were sent up at short intervals; the number is unknown but Rowe said that there were a couple left in a box when the signalling was abandoned, so probably 18 to 22 were fired.

About 25 minutes before the firework display began, Boxhall and many others aboard the stricken liner had spotted the masthead lights of another steamer only about five or 10 miles away, off the port bow. Like the mystery ship seen from *Californian*, this vessel studiously ignored all attempts to contact her.

Away on the liner's starboard side was another vessel, a sailing ship, seen by J. Bruce Ismay. This vessel, now tentatively identified

as the *Lady St Johns*, was a small two-masted ship on her way to Newfoundland. She was becalmed and unable to offer any assistance even though her crew were aware that there was something amiss.

The first lifeboat usually believed to have left *Titanic* was Number 7, lowered at 12.45am. Not enough first class women and children could be found to fill the boat so it was lowered with just 28 aboard, three of them crewmen. Undoubtedly more people could have been found to fill the boat if the officers had not construed the 'women and children first' tradition as 'women and children only', or if third class had been given a chance to reach it. But many of the third class passengers were being prevented from reaching the boat deck by locked doors, iron grilles and officers brandishing revolvers, which they were not afraid to use.

Twenty-eight people including two male passengers and two crew-members were crammed into Boat 6, designed to hold 65, and hurriedly lowered away at about 12.50am. The two crewmen, Hitchens and Fleet, not being seamen, were unable to manage the lifeboat so Arthur Peuchen, an amateur yachtsman, was allowed by Lightoller to slide down the ropes to the boat, to lend a hand. Even with the intrepid yachtsman's help Fleet and Hitchens could not row the boat on their own, so the female passengers aboard were pressed into helping out.

Five minutes later Boat 5 was lowered, with just 39 people in it. Then it was Number 3's turn to be loaded by Mr Murdoch. Lifeboat 3 is interesting because it appeared to be an old one taken from another ship; at least that is what the seaman asked about its condition by Mrs Frederick Speddon thought. All the rest of the boats seem to have been marked with their respective numbers, but this particular lifeboat, uniquely, carried both 5 and 3. No fewer than 50 persons made their escape in Number 3: 25 women and children, 10 male passengers and 15 members of the liner's crew were on board when it left at 1.00am.

Next came private hire Boat 1, the forward starboard emergency boat that should have been carried away or wrecked by the iceberg. Sir Cosmo Duff Gordon, his wife, her secretary and two American friends, climbed into the boat; they were joined by seven members of the crew, to do the rowing, before Mr Murdoch ordered the boat lowered. Sir Cosmo later paid the seamen £5 apiece, ostensibly to replace the kit they had been obliged to leave aboard the ship. Boat 1 left *Titanic* at about 1.10am, the most extreme example of self help evident that night.

Boat 8 was loading at about the same time as Number 1, to a similar criterion. Second Officer Lightoller allowed only women and children to board the boat, and even those from third class were excluded. Steward John Hart, one of the very few crewmen aboard *Titanic* to consider the safety of third class passengers, brought a group of about 30 of them to the boat, only to have them turned away by Lightoller. At 1.10am Boat 8 was lowered away with just 28 people in it, four of them members of the crew.

By this time the ship's list to starboard had become more pronounced, which meant that the starboard boats were swinging well clear of the side of the hull whilst those on the other side were

The

# HEROIC MUSICIANS OF THE TITANIC
who died at their posts like men ~ April 15th 1912

G. KRINS. Violin.

W. HARTLEY.
BANDMASTER.

R. BRICOUX. Cello.

W.T. BRAILEY. Piano

J.W. WOODWARD. Cello.

P.C. TAYLOR. Piano

Nearer, my God, to Thee.

Or if on joyful wing cleaving the sky,
Sun, moon and stars forgot, upwards I fly,
Still all my song shall be,
Nearer, my GOD, to Thee, nearer to Thee.

Nature might stand up,
And say to all the world,
This was a man.

J.F.C. CLARKE. Bass

J.L. HUME. Violin.

*Left:* As *Titanic* was sinking, the members of the band assembled on deck and played light popular music in an effort to calm frightened passengers. They continued to play until long after all of the lifeboats were gone and the decks, as the ship's bows sank, tilted to an angle where they could no longer keep their feet. At the last moment the band stopped playing popular music and instead played Bandmaster Wallace Hartley's favourite hymn 'Nearer My God To Thee'. All of the band members were lost.

*Right:* Bandmaster Wallace Hartley as a very young man.

bumping against the steel plates. Boat 9 seems to have been mainly loaded from A deck, and the women and children that boarded it had to jump across the gap between it and the ship's side. Some made the attempt successfully, others made it into the boat but injured themselves in the process, some females couldn't bring themselves to leap across the yawning chasm and fled. Many male passengers were only too ready to make the jump but Purser McElroy had foreseen this problem and had stationed three crewmen in the boat to deal with it. They were not wholly successful. When, at 1.20am, Number 9 was lowered there were 56 persons aboard: 42 women and children, eight crew-members and six male passengers.

A sense of real urgency had overtaken events aboard and just five minutes later Boat 11 was lowered away. Officers Murdoch and Moody had at last got one right. There were 69 or 70 people in the boat, four or five more than it was designed to carry. At about the same time Number 10 was also lowered, with 55 people in it.

Below decks chaos reigned. Officers with guns tried to stop third class passengers from reaching the boat deck, where they might prevent the more deserving first class from finding lifeboat places. The predominantly Italian catering staff, employed by Gatti's, were confined in the second class dining saloon. They were still there when the ship sank an hour later.

Groups of male passengers were trying to rush the boats and only determined efforts by the crew prevented them. Even so, when Boat 12 was lowered with just 43 people aboard, a desperate Frenchman supposedly leapt into it from B deck. This would have been impossible if B deck had in fact been converted to having extra cabin space. At the same time Thomas Andrews and Stewards Edward Wheelton and James Widgery were roaming back and forth along B deck, making sure that passengers were out of their cabins. Whilst engaged in these perambulations Wheelton noticed that Boat 11 was still hanging from its davits, again indicating that the outside part of B deck was an open promenade.

The threat, and almost certainly use, of firearms was required to keep panicking male passengers out of Boat 14. Fifth Officer Lowe needed little encouragement to use his revolver, or to ensure that there was room in the lifeboat for himself. A youngster, 'hardly more than a schoolboy', found his way into the boat, but he was spotted by Lowe. The Fifth Officer threatened to shoot the youth if he did not leave the boat immediately. With no alternative, the youth did

as he was told. After allowing six crew-members into the boat, including himself, Lowe had it lowered. There were 64 people in Boat 14, including Lowe and an Italian stowaway. Mr Lowe, at least, was relatively safe, which is more than can be said for the boy. Ironically, the boat was intended to carry 65 persons, so there was one empty seat.

As Boat 14 was lowered away Lowe fired another three shots to deter anybody who might be contemplating jumping into the boat. When the boat was about 5ft above the water there was some trouble with the tackle used to lower it. Possibly the sailors above had retreated from the hail of gunfire. Unable to wait for the problem to be sorted out, Lowe pulled the lever of the Murray's Patented Release Gear, designed to release both ends of the lifeboat from its ropes simultaneously. The boat fell the last 5ft into the water and consequently leaked like a sieve for the rest of the night.

The next boat away was Number 16, the aft port lifeboat. As it was lowered away at about 1.35am, the 56 people in it could hear

*Titanic's* band, led by Wallace Hartley, playing in a gallant attempt to calm the passengers. The heroic musicians, with no thought for their own safety, continued to play right up to the end.

Over on the starboard side of the ship Boat 13 was the next attended to by Sixth Officer Moody. By the time it was lowered there were 63 people in it, including nine crewmen and three stewardesses. Watching from the boat deck was second class passenger Lawrence Beesley, a schoolteacher. A seaman in the boat looked up, saw Beesley, and asked him if there were any more women or children on the boat deck. The schoolmaster replied that there were not, and was promptly invited to jump into the boat, which he did. (Beesley, who wrote possibly the best survivor account of the sinking, died on 14 April 1967,

*Right, top to bottom:*

Hartley as he looked at the time of the *Titanic* disaster.

John (Jock) Hume; violinist aboard *Titanic*.

J. F. C. Clarke; bass player.

*Below:* **During the early stages of the voyage *Titanic's* eight-piece band had regularly entertained first and second class passengers playing selections from the official White Star music book.**

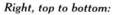

exactly 55 years after the disaster.) Another important witness who made his escape in Boat 13 was Reginald Lee, one of the lookouts who had first reported the iceberg ahead of the ship. Although he never mentioned it at either the British or American inquiries, Lee later told his family that he saw at least one lifeboat capsized, and another sunk. This assertion is supported by the captains of both ships at the scene the following morning.

Moments after Boat 13 had reached the water it was Number 15's turn. There was no longer any pretence of discipline amongst the male passengers, and a group of them tried to rush the lifeboat. They were beaten back by the crew, 14 of whom promptly clambered into the boat themselves. They allowed 53 third class female passengers to join them along with one first class (sic) male before the boat was lowered.

Lightoller next turned his attention to Emergency Boat 2, while Murdoch got Collapsible Boat C under the davits vacated by Boat 3. A crowd of passengers, described by surviving officers as 'Italians and foreigners', sneaked into the collapsible and were forcibly removed at gunpoint by Murdoch. *Titanic's* officers were quite prepared to use their firearms and Seamen Jack Williams and William French saw at least six male passengers shot. Third class passenger Eugene Daly saw the bodies of a couple of passengers who, he was informed, had been shot. Murdoch collected up all of the women and children he could find, 27 in all, and herded them into the collapsible boat. He then allowed just two first class male passengers to board, supposedly without knowing who they were. Wealthy Philadelphian William Carter and Joseph Bruce Ismay took their seats amongst the third class women. Lurking in the bottom of the boat, unseen by Mr Murdoch, were four Chinese who had managed to steal aboard. At 1.40am Boat C left the ship.

When Lightoller reached Emergency Boat 2, to begin loading it, he found it already full with what he described as 'dagoes'. It did not take the second officer long to clear the boat, with the aid of his trusty revolver, to make room for what he considered a more suitable complement. Three crewmen, under the command of Fourth Officer Boxhall, were allowed into the boat along with eight first class female passengers, one old man and his family from third class and eight or nine third class women. At about 1.45am Collapsible C was lowered away with just 25 people in a boat that

*Left: La Provence*, **which received** *Titanic's* **first distress call at 12.15am.**

*Below:* **Roger Bricoux; cellist.**

should have held 40. Fortunately Joseph Boxhall had the foresight to take a box of green flares with him. These would not only allow the rest of the boats to keep Number 2 in sight but would also give any potential rescuer a much greater chance of sighting the otherwise unlit boats. There should have been a lantern and compass in each of the lifeboats, but in fact there were none.

Boat 4 was still swinging about outside on A deck, but someone had at last managed to get the windows open. The sounding spar had been cut away, so there was now nothing to stop the boat from being lowered. At 1.55am Number 4 creaked down, with just 34 first class female passengers, one French stowaway and five crewmen. John Jacob Astor had asked Lightoller for permission to join his wife in the boat as it was being loaded. Permission was refused. Lightoller obviously believed that it was better for the boat to depart with 25 vacant seats than for one extra male passenger to escape the sinking ship.

Collapsible D was now supposedly the last boat still aboard that could be got under davits. The other two collapsibles, A and B, were stored on the roof of the 'officers' house' where the rigging for the forward funnel would make it difficult, but not impossible, to move them on to the main boat deck.

Three crewmen were allowed into D, apparently all there were available. There also seems to have been a desperate shortage of third class women and children so Lightoller had to make do with 37 first class ones. A third class male passenger managed to stow away aboard. The boat was lowered at about 2.05am, and on the way down two more male passengers leapt into it. Yet another male passenger, Frederick Hoyt, whose wife was already in the boat, tried to jump in but missed. As soon as Collapsible D reached the water he was hauled aboard.

The ship was sinking fast by now and the forecastle head was just

**Virginian picked up the last faint wireless signal from Titanic at 2.17am, presumably when electrical power aboard the liner finally failed.**

disappearing beneath the water as the last boats, A and B, were wrestled towards the davits. Boat A was first over the side, with whoever could scramble aboard it. The only passenger known to have been in A when it was launched shortly after 2.05am was August Wennerstrom.

There was no time for niceties such as raising the canvas sides of Boat B before it was lowered. It would have to serve as it was. As water swept back over the forecastle, B was hurriedly swung over the side and lowering began. For some reason, perhaps the tackle jammed or broke, one end of the boat went down faster than the other until it was hanging vertically, tipping its occupants into the sea. There was no more time.

In the wireless cabin Jack Phillips was still at his post trying to summon aid. Harold Bride, probably at Phillips' direction, had already left to seek a place in one of the boats. Despite Bride's testimony that he and Phillips left the wireless room together, at the captain's orders, sometime round about 2.10am, Titanic's feeble last wireless signal was picked up by the SS Virginian at 2.17am. By that time the wireless cabin was already submerged, and who but Phillips could have been operating the transmitter?

Captain Smith, as far as can be ascertained, was on the bridge of his ship during the last few minutes she remained afloat.

At about 2.15am Titanic's stern began to lift out of the water as her bows sank. Passengers and crew alike scrambled towards the rear of the ship in an attempt to prolong their lives by a minute or two. The last boat, B, was torn from its tackle, as the ship's bow sank ever deeper, and floated free but upside down. There were already people who had fallen, jumped, or been washed overboard from the ship and some of these quickly struggled on to the capsized boat, amongst them Charles Lightoller, John Hagan and Harold Bride. All three men had been trying to get the boat free when the sea had completed the task for them.

The band, which had been steadily playing light music throughout, now struck up a hymn 'Nearer My God to Thee', the bandmaster's favourite. From the lifeboats people could see a green glow coming from the submerged part of the ship as the lights continued to burn underwater. People were jumping overboard in ever greater numbers as the ship began to slide forward, her stern rising. Then the forward funnel collapsed, crushing the starboard bridge wing and narrowly missing Boat A floating close by. The forward motion stopped and the stern began to rise more quickly into the air until about 150ft of the hull rose vertically from the sea.

In Boat 13 Lawrence Beesley watched as 'she tilted slowly up, revolving apparently about a centre of gravity just astern of amidships, until she attained a vertically upright position and there

enough to re-board it, by which time the boat was once more floating the right way up but was full of water. All that was keeping it afloat was the buoyancy ring around the wooden bottom and the tanks in bow and stern. Even so, for a while the damaged collapsible provided some hope for about 30 people. As with Boat B, all of the people aboard had been in the freezing water and had very little resistance to the cold remaining. Before first light more than half of those aboard A had succumbed and only 14 remained alive, accompanied by three corpses.

Boat 4 was still close by after the ship sank and the occupants managed to pull seven people out of the water, all crewmen, but two of these died from the cold even though they had been immersed for only a couple of minutes at most.

*Olympic* had left New York at about 3.00pm on Saturday 13 April, on the homeward leg of her voyage. She first picked up a distress signal from the *Titanic* at 1.00am on the 15th. Minutes after receiving the distress call Captain Haddock was heading at full speed towards *Titanic*, but the distance was too great for there to be any hope of reaching the stricken vessel in time to be of any help. *Carpathia* was also racing to the scene and would arrive at about daybreak.

Throughout the hours of darkness the people in the boats did what they could to help themselves. Some of them rowed towards the lights of the mysterious steamer, which was still visible but keeping her distance. As the boats moved towards her so the stranger moved away. In other boats the people just rowed in an effort to keep warm. In Boat 2 Fourth Officer Boxhall systematically lit his green flares so that the other boats could home in on them instead of scattering in the darkness. Fifth Officer Lowe, in Boat 14, began to round up as many of the other boats as he could and tie them together. Once he had collected Boats 10, 12, 16 and D, Lowe began to move people from his own boat into the others and to put together a hand-picked crew for Boat 14 ready to return to the site of the sinking in search of survivors. By the time he was ready, about an hour after *Titanic* had foundered, the other boats in his little flotilla were all heavily loaded, D to the point where it was in danger of sinking. To make matters worse for the unhappy occupants of Boat D, Lowe had left them without any crewmen to row and the boat was drifting helplessly.

By the time Lowe returned to the site of the sinking it was too late for most of those who had gone into the water. Although a search was made, only four people were found alive and one of these, Steward J. Stewart, died soon after being taken aboard Number 14.

she remained motionless. As she swung up, her lights, which had shone without a flicker all night, went out suddenly, came on again for a single flash, then went out altogether.' The time the lights went out can be fixed by the last wireless message received by *Virginian*, as 2.17am.

The ship remained in a vertical position for some minutes before gently sliding under the surface at about 2.20am.

## The Rescue

When *Titanic* foundered hundreds of people were thrown into the water. Most would have died instantly from the shock of being suddenly immersed in water at -2°C. Those who survived would have only a couple of minutes before the cold immobilised and then killed them.

Collapsible Boats A and B were still close enough for some swimmers to reach. Between 30 and 40 climbed on to upturned Boat B where Second Officer Lightoller took charge. To keep the capsized craft stable the people aboard were obliged to stand back to back on the upturned bottom. In this manner they passed the hours of darkness but before dawn came many died from the effects of the cold and were pushed overboard.

The invasion of Collapsible A was not so orderly and a great mass of people tried to scramble aboard. The collapsible sides were wrecked and the whole boat was overturned. Its original occupants were thrown into the sea and only August Wennerstrom was lucky

*Top:* The sight that met the eyes of those aboard *Carpathia* in the first light of 16 April. The iceberg shown cannot be the one struck by *Titanic* as there is no part of it that could have overhung the liner's forward well deck.

*Above: Carpathia's* passengers and crew gazing at the immense field of ice that had proved so lethal to *Titanic*.

While Lowe was away from his flotilla of lifeboats it began to get light and crewman Fred Clench, in Boat 12, spotted what looked like a life-raft with a group of people on it. He heard two blasts on an officer's whistle from the raft. Clench called to the officer, who turned out to be Charles Lightoller. Lightoller requested that Number 12 be rowed over to them and that they be taken off the upturned collapsible. Lightoller immediately took command of Number 12 and, master mariner that he was, redistributed the occupants so as to make the small boat ride high by the bows. Consequently, the people in Number 12 spent the remainder of their time in the boat struggling to prevent it sinking by the stern.

As the coming dawn began to lighten the sky the people in the boats caught sight of rockets away to the southeast. *Carpathia* was coming to their rescue. Boxhall in Boat 2 set off one of his few remaining flares to let the Cunarder know exactly where they were. The flares were seen and at about 4.00am *Carpathia* stopped to begin taking aboard the survivors from Boxhall's boat. As it grew

fully light the survivors in their lifeboats and the seamen aboard *Carpathia* were met by a truly awe-inspiring sight. All around them were dozens of immense icebergs, stretching as far as the eye could see, at least 25 of them standing 200ft above the water. Only superb seamanship, diligent lookouts and a great deal of luck, had saved *Carpathia* from sharing *Titanic's* fate. Slowly the Cunard liner moved from lifeboat to lifeboat taking aboard first the survivors and then, in most cases, the boats themselves. As well as the ice, Captain Rostron could clearly see two more steamers, neither of them *Californian*, about seven or eight miles to the north of where he had found the lifeboats.

Boat 14's adventures were not yet over. Lowe had managed to raise a mast and sail on the lifeboat, and had everything well under control. He had taken the badly overloaded Collapsible D in tow and was heading for *Carpathia* when he spotted what looked like a life-raft with about 20 people on it. Lowe headed for the raft and took off the people but apparently didn't take a great deal of notice of the craft itself. Luckily, Joseph Scarrott did take notice of the raft. He described it as 'constructed of air boxes. It was not a collapsible boat.' Scarrott's description is important inasmuch as *Titanic* did not carry any such rafts. Nor could Scarrott have mistaken the raft for waterlogged Collapsible A. Shortly after picking up the raft's survivors, as Number 14 was again towing Collapsible D towards *Carpathia*, they came across Collapsible A. The 12 survivors in this waterlogged boat were so far gone that Lowe had to fire four shots over their heads to wake them up. Leaving three corpses and a number of rings taken from people who had died aboard A, Lowe set off once more towards *Carpathia*.

By 8.00am all 705 of *Titanic's* survivors were aboard *Carpathia*, seemingly along with 135 survivors, whose names do not appear on *Titanic's* crew or passenger lists, from somewhere else. These extra 135 people are named in the lists of survivors transmitted by *Carpathia* a little later. As well as picking up the people, Captain Rostron had also picked up 13 White Star lifeboats, Numbers 1, 2, 3, 5, 6, 7, 8, 9, 10, 11, 12, 13 and 16. Collapsibles A and B were simply abandoned, while Boats 4, 14, 15, C and D were scuttled.

As *Carpathia* was collecting the last of the survivors the *Californian* joined them. During the night a series of white rockets had been seen from the *Californian's* bridge but they did not go high enough or make enough noise for the officers to think that they might be distress signals. They believed that the rockets were merely one ship passing a message to another, a common practice.

Captain Lord had left instructions that he was to be awakened at first light and First Officer Stewart duly woke him at about 4.30am. Even after Lord had reached the bridge he did not immediately get his ship under way but waited until there was enough light to see the best route through the icefield. At about 5.15am *Californian* finally began to pick her way through the ice in a westerly direction. Only then did the first officer draw the captain's attention to a four-masted steamer to their south and inform him of the rockets seen during the night. For the first time Captain Lord had reason to believe that another ship might be in trouble. He immediately gave orders that the wireless operator should be wakened and should contact any other ships in the area to find out if anything was wrong. Evans' first signal brought a reply from the *Frankfurt* telling him that *Titanic* had sunk during the night. *Frankfurt's* message was followed by another, from the *Virginian*, confirming the news and giving *Titanic's* last known position. Captain Lord altered course, through the ice, and headed towards where the White Star liner had sunk.

By the time *Californian* arrived at the scene of the sinking there was very little she could do to help. Captain Rostron had decided to return to New York with his load of survivors, and so that he could leave the scene without delay he asked Captain Lord to search the area for any more survivors. Captain Lord obliged, and in doing so took note of the lifeboats Captain Rostron had abandoned. Amongst the floating ice were two upturned boats, one a collapsible which should have been there, and one a full sized wooden lifeboat that should not. Captain Rostron had also noted the capsized extra proper lifeboat. *Californian* found no more survivors to rescue.

As *Carpathia* headed for New York the cover-up of what had really happened to *Titanic* began in earnest aboard her. A note requesting that they make no statement, in any detail, when they arrived was circulated amongst the survivors. As a result of the circulation of this note, not one in 10 would submit to questioning once they arrived in America. A survivor committee led by Samuel Goldenberg, a first-class passenger from *Titanic*, issued other decrees, which display technical knowledge of which ordinary

*Left:* **Captain Arthur H. Rostron of the *Carpathia*, as he appeared at the official inquiries into the loss of the *Titanic*.**

*Below:* **A lifeboat swinging from its davits, exactly as it would have appeared on *Californian* as she steamed towards *Titanic's* last known position on the morning of 15 April 1912.**

S.S. Californian. (Allan Line.)

*Above: Carpathia* at New York.

*Left:* The Leyland cargo passenger vessel *Californian*, which was long thought to have been the mystery ship visible from *Titanic* as she sank.

*Above right: Californian* lying stopped in ice, with Captain Stanley Lord (inset). *Californian* was 19 1/2 miles away from *Titanic* while she was sinking, well beyond the limits of visibility.

*Right: Carpathia* berthed at Liverpool shortly after her return to normal service following the *Titanic* disaster.

passengers would have been ignorant. Clearly these decrees were the work of people who understood ships such as Ismay, Rostron and perhaps other officers aboard. It is interesting to note that the majority of these so-called decrees were not supported by the great majority of the survivors, being signed solely by the 25 members of the committee.

It is widely known that the American scout cruisers *Chester* and *Salem* were sent, on President Taft's explicit instructions, to intercept *Carpathia* and gather all possible information, without any great success. It is not quite so well known that these were not the only American vessels sent to meet the Cunarder. A revenue cutter, either *Mohawk* or *Seneca* was despatched from New York, and another, the

*Gresham*, from Boston. These vessels had no more luck than the scout cruisers. Even personal messages from US President Taft and Guglielmo Marconi could not persuade *Carpathia's* wireless operators to divulge any information about the fate of *Titanic*. Secretly, Marconi's Chief Engineer in New York, Frederick M. Sammis, sent a total of four messages to Cottam on *Carpathia* instructing him to keep quiet until after the ship reached port.

At about 6.00pm on Thursday 18 April *Carpathia* entered New York harbour. Although surrounded by press boats, Captain Rostron would allow no reporters on to his vessel. Instead of proceeding to her own berth she first went to the White Star pier and dropped *Titanic's* lifeboats off. Then Rostron made his way to the Cunard pier and prepared to disgorge his load of survivors.

Landing Stage, Liverpool.

## UNSINKABLE LIFE-BOATS.

An unsinkable life-boat, unsinkable even though seriously damaged, is the product of a Danish inventor, and several important features are claimed for the new craft.

This life-boat consists of a boat-shaped pontoon of wood or iron, strongly constructed, and filled with kapok, a product of plants growing in Java and Sumatra, said to combine the greatest floating capacity with the least weight and able to sustain thirty-five times its weight in water. The kapok is contained in water-tight cushions which in turn are placed in water-tight compartments. Upon this buoyant layer is mounted a superstructure which can be folded down or erected. This is surrounded by a fender filled with kapok in water-tight cushions. In extending the boat, cross

**Unsinkable Lifeboat Extended for Use**

beams are lifted in and the oars are released, an oval-shaped thwart with crossthwarts slides into position, and stanchions and other parts drop into their places automatically, making a reliable boat containing bread and water-tanks.

Exhaustive tests have been made of the Englehardt unsinkable life-boat, as it is called, and it has stood successfully every one. It is compact for carrying on vessels, where space occupied is an important consideration, and if a ship were to sink suddenly these boats would only need be cut from their lashings and would be

**The Boat Folded.**

found floating after such disaster, still fit for use and easily accessible by those in danger of perishing. The boats can, moreover, be readily transported to any part of a ship and launched without davits.

The ordinary lifeboats take up so much deck space that it is impossible to carry enough for passengers and crew, and as a consequence the boats are apt to be overcrowded and swamped.

*Right:* Englehardt collapsible lifeboats. *Titanic* carried four of these boats, two of which, at least, were properly launched and saved 83 people. The other two collapsible boats were supposedly washed overboard as the ship sank and were used as rafts. Almost 40 people were saved by the second two Englehart boats.

*Below:* Fifth Officer Harold Lowe, who was more than ready to use his firearm to keep order. Lowe is something of a contradictory character. On the one hand he ordered a boy out of Boat 4 before leaving *Titanic* in that same boat. On the other he is the only officer to take his lifeboat back to where *Titanic* had sunk in a search for survivors in the water.

Ostensibly to protect the survivors from prying newspaper reporters, the streets leading to the docks were barricaded, and the pier itself was roped off for 25yd either side of the main entrance. Only a maximum of two close relatives for any survivor were allowed on to the pier, and these were not encouraged to board *Carpathia*. One of the few people who was allowed to board the rescue ship soon after its arrival at New York was Guglielmo Marconi, who was on hand to look after the interests of his employees Cottam and Bride. Accompanying Marconi was a *New York Times* reporter, Jim Spears. The newspaper was prepared to pay the wireless operators handsomely for their version of the tragedy.

The American government, in order to lessen the stress of arriving in a new country, had suspended all customs regulations for *Titanic's* survivors. Shortly before 10.00pm the survivors began to leave the ship. As always, everything was strictly controlled and they were allowed ashore only in order of class, with first going first. After all of the passengers had left the ship, and the quayside was almost deserted, *Titanic's* surviving crew-members filed down the Cunarder's sternmost gangway and were led along the pier. They were taken down a narrow flight of stairs to where the US Immigration Service tender *George Starr* awaited them. The tender took the crew six blocks to the north, to White Star Pier 60, where they were shepherded aboard another I.M.M. ship, the Red Star Line's *Lapland*. Here the majority of the surviving crew would remain, incommunicado, until *Lapland* returned them to their home shores.

During the night all identifying marks, such as numbers and White Star motifs, were removed from the lifeboats, ostensibly to deter souvenir hunters. On the following day *Titanic's* name was sanded off the boats. On the Saturday they were lifted out of the water, hoisted into a loft and covered with a tarpaulin.

*Right:* Anxious friends and relatives surround the White Star Line's New York offices awaiting news, with (inset) *Titanic's* second wireless operator, Harold Bride, giving a version of events to the American inquiry.

# THE
# SINKING
## of the
# TITANIC

*I*N the picture on the right, the wireless operator is undergoing examination as to the time the S O S messages were sent out. And below is the crowd surrounding the White Star offices in a despairing effort to obtain the very latest news of the catastrophe.

*Photos : S. and G.*

# SEARCHING FOR SCAPEGOATS

The official American inquiry into the loss of the *Titanic* began on the day *Carpathia* arrived in New York when Senator William Alden Smith, who headed the inquiry, visited her. He was there for a half hour interview with J. Bruce Ismay and I.M.M.'s Vice President, Phillip A. S. Franklin. What transpired at the interview has never been disclosed but, whatever it was, it set the scene for two of the most inept official inquiries on record.

Senator Smith's primary objective should have been to discover the cause of the disaster and thereby guard against the same thing ever happening again. He also, apparently, wanted to show that the officers and crew of the *Titanic* had been negligent and that the company was aware of this, which of course they were. He failed hopelessly on all counts. Nevertheless, he did manage to acquire a good deal of personal publicity, which is never a bad thing as far as politicians are concerned.

Despite appearing to interrogate an exhausted J. Bruce Ismay, the senator could get no indication of negligence on the part of the company. Neither did the surviving *Titanic's* officers tell of negligence aboard the ship. Second Officer Charles Lightoller, Fifth Officer Lowe and Second Wireless Operator Harold Bride all told heroic stories, almost certainly untrue. The rank and file of the crew, if they were questioned at all, were interviewed by individual members of the seven-man inquiry committee, three at a time. Anything they said that did not fit in with what the inquiry wanted to hear was simply ignored.

By the time the inquiry was three days old it was evident that it was going nowhere. They were going to need a scapegoat, and during the session on Monday 22 April, Fourth Officer Joseph Boxhall, *Titanic's* navigating officer, pointed the way when he made the first mention of a mystery ship. The presence of a mysterious vessel which failed to come to the aid of the sinking liner was confirmed by other witnesses and the search for this vessel began.

On 24 April Ernest Gill, a crew-member from the *Californian*, sold a story identifying her as the mystery ship to a Boston newspaper for $500. The story was obviously a fabrication simply intended to earn its author a useful sum of money, but it did provide the Smith inquiry with a target.

Supposedly in the interests of fair play, Captain Lord and the watch officers of the *Californian* were called to give evidence. Lord gave his ship's position throughout the sinking as $19^1/_2$ miles from *Titanic*, and told of the repeated attempts of his officers to contact the ship they had in view by Morse lamp. None of his officers denied that they had seen rockets at about the time *Titanic* was sinking, but they did say that they thought they were not distress signals. Nobody on *Californian* could positively say just what sort of ship they did see, but they did all agree that this vessel, whatever it might have been, was under way. As *Titanic* never moved during the time a mystery ship was visible from *Californian* it is reasonable to suppose that the ship observed was not the White Star liner. Notwithstanding this clear evidence of Lord's innocence, Senator Smith had found his scapegoat.

The sham dragged on until 19 May before Senator Smith was prepared to make his report; a report that has been misleading people ever since. The report contained a description of the ship, her owners, and her truncated trials. The voyage prior to the collision was covered, as was the collision and progressive sinking of the liner. Only a brief summary of the wireless traffic following the collision was given. The senator also criticised the British Board of Trade for its outdated regulations that allowed so large a ship to operate with insufficient lifeboats. (A red herring that has deflected serious investigators until the present time.)

Captain Smith was censured for his indifference to danger. This was the only possible cause of the disaster that William Smith recognised. And anyway, Captain Smith was a safe target as he was unable to defend himself, having gone down with the ship.

Captain Lord of the *Californian* was condemned for failing to go to the assistance of a vessel in trouble. Despite this sweeping condemnation, Captain Lord never received any sort of communication on the subject from the American inquiry. Smith had made the most of his scapegoat. Twenty-three years after the event, *Titanic's* senior surviving officer, Charles Lightoller, described the American inquiry as 'a farce'.

The *Lapland* entered Plymouth harbour, with 172 of *Titanic's* surviving crew-members aboard, on the morning of 29 April. The crew-members expected to be allowed to go home. Their hopes were soon dashed. Instead, they were imprisoned, behind locked gates, in Plymouth dockyard's third class waiting room. Dockyard police and local constabulary patrolled the outside of the waiting room to make sure that the crew spoke to nobody. Before being released the survivors would be interviewed by the Receiver of Wrecks, and then asked to give their word of honour that they would not talk publicly about what had happened. Despite this pledge of secrecy, some survivors did manage to exchange a few words with the reporters waiting outside the gates of their prison. Realising that the word of honour system was not working, a government agent who happened to be present compelled the survivors to sign the Official Secrets Act. If they spoke out of turn after signing that document they would be liable to the most extreme punishments.

Only when the survivors had been interrogated, and had signed the Official Secrets Act, were they were allowed to leave Plymouth in groups. About 85 seamen, firemen, lookouts, greasers, etc, left the dockyard and were put on a special train for Southampton in the evening of the first day. The rest were released the following day.

Forty three of *Titanic's* crew were still in America, giving evidence before the Smith inquiry. As these completed their evidence in dribs and drabs they were allowed to leave for home. The last of these, Harold Bride, finally reached the shores of Britain on 18 May, more than a month after the sinking.

Although nobody knew it, there was still one survivor to be accounted for, Fireman Thomas Hart. Hart turned up at his home in College Street, Southampton, at about the same time as Bride arrived back in Britain. As he had not been amongst the survivors picked up by *Carpathia*, Hart had some explaining to do. The unlikely story he told was that he had lost his papers in a Southampton pub shortly before *Titanic* had sailed and somebody else must have taken his place on the ship. To account for the missing month he claimed to have been living rough, afraid to return home. As no fewer than 34 other members of *Titanic's* 'black gang' lived close to Hart and would have recognised him, any impostor taking Hart's place on the ship would have been exposed immediately he claimed to be the fireman. Thomas Hart's name does not appear on the list of seamen who, having been signed on as crew, failed to join the ship before she sailed. Somebody sailed as Thomas Hart, almost certainly the man himself!

The Board of Trade was understandably keen to conduct the official British inquiry. After all, it was its obsolete regulations that had allowed the ship to leave Southampton with far too few lifeboats for the number of people who could be carried aboard. It was its inspector who had allowed the ship to leave Southampton with a fire blazing in Number 10 bunker. What better means of controlling the inquiry's findings than to be both plaintiff and defendant?

To ensure that the inquiry went along the lines most favourable to the Board it would need to be headed by someone who had considerable experience in not exposing anything too embarrassing. John Charles Bigham, Baron Mersey of Toxteth, who had already demonstrated his ability to cover up shady government dealings, was selected. Mersey had been party to the inquiry into, and cover-up of, the infamous Jameson Raid that had helped spark off the Boer War. He would have five assessors, all experienced in various maritime matters, to assist him. A venue was selected, the Drill Hall of the London Scottish Regiment, notorious for its appalling acoustics. Even though the hall was large enough to accommodate 300 people, none of them would be able to hear clearly what was said. Not until all of the witnesses had given their evidence was this venue belatedly changed. The inquiry, if that is the right word, began on 2 May and would not end until 30 July when Lord Mersey presented his own report.

The British inquiry ran along similar lines to the American

inquiry inasmuch as witnesses were carefully selected, as were the questions they would be asked and who would do the asking. Interestingly, counsel who should have been representing the interests of Captain Lord and the *Californian* was effectively barred from doing so by continual interruption by Lord Mersey. Captain Lord was to be given no chance at all to defend or explain himself.

With consummate skill Mersey controlled witnesses, allowing them to say only what he wanted to hear. If a witness did manage to say something the chairman did not like he simply ignored or misinterpreted it. He even went so far as to badger witnesses into changing their testimony until it fitted in with his preconceived ideas, but no longer said what the witness intended. Like the American inquiry, the British one was a farce, but a farce with a vindictive edge.

Robert Hitchens, *Titanic's* helmsman, testified that red, white and blue rockets were fired, and that starboard rudder was not applied either before or after the collision.

*Right: Titanic's* **second wireless operator Harold Bride who, after much persuasion, assisted *Carpathia's* wireless operator, Cottam, in transmitting the names of the 705 *Titanic* survivors, and another 135 who seem to have come from somewhere else.**

*Below:* **Harold Bride being carried ashore from *Carpathia* at New York. His feet, as well as being frost-bitten, were supposedly wrenched when he caught them in the slats at the bottom of the lifeboat.**

William Lucas told how third class were left to their own devices. Reginald Lee told that the point of impact was just forward of the foremast, not at the bow. Lee and Fred Fleet told how the berg was shrouded in mist. Robert Dillon testified how he had been ordered to tell the firemen to keep steam up. Lord Mersey ignored them all.

Steward Alfred Crawford told the inquiry how, as his lifeboat was leaving *Titanic*, 'Captain Smith ordered us to make for the lights (about five to seven miles away), hand over the passengers and then come back to the ship.' As it was impossible for anybody to have rowed a lifeboat the 10 or 12 miles needed to complete Smith's orders, in the time available, then the captain must have expected that the ship whose lights could be seen from *Titanic* would close that distance dramatically. Contact with this mystery vessel was never established, as Captain Smith would have known. A possible reason he could have had for expecting the ship to come closer was that there was already some arrangement for it to do so. This implication was so obvious that even Lord Mersey could not ignore it; instead he chose to change the evidence. He suggested that what Captain Smith had really said was, 'Go to that light, put your passengers off and return to this place.' Whose evidence is more likely to be correct; that of a witness who was there or that of a judge who was not?

When Thomas Lewis, acting for the British Seafarers' Union, attempted to question Crawford, Mersey intervened. Taking the counsel's notes from him Lord Mersey took over the questioning himself, so denying counsel and witness the freedom to reveal the facts. Unsurprisingly Lord Mersey's questioning elicited no useful information.

Captains Lord and Rostron both told that there were more lifeboats at the scene of the sinking than the White Star liner had actually carried. The information escaped Lord Mersey's attention, or at least it appeared to.

With no intention whatsoever of trying to find out what had actually caused the loss of the *Titanic*, Lord Mersey set about diverting attention by destroying the reputation of Captain Stanley Lord.

Captain Lord gave his evidence on day seven of the inquiry. He gave the position of the *Californian* when she stopped for the night, soon after 10.00pm on 14 April, 19 1/2 miles from *Titanic*. He described the vessel he saw approach them, and how and why he was sure it was not a large liner. Lord explained how the mystery ship had moved during the night when both *Californian* and *Titanic* were stationary.

When Captain Lord told the inquiry that one of the reasons he did not know, at the time, about the rockets seen from his ship was that it was 2.00am and he was sleeping, Attorney General Sir Rufus Isaacs said that he found it impossible to believe the captain was asleep at that hour! Isaacs was not really the person to comment on what was normal

R.M.S. CEDRIC, (WHITE STAR LINE,) 21,035 TONS.

*Above:* The White Star liner *Cedric*. While he was aboard the *Carpathia* J. Bruce Ismay sent a wireless message to the White Star officers in New York ordering them to keep *Cedric* there so that all of *Titanic's* surviving crew could be sent home immediately they arrived. Because of the pending American inquiry, Ismay's orders were ignored.

*Right:* The Waldorf Astoria Hotel, New York, where the American inquiry into the loss of the *Titanic* was held.

behaviour as at the time of the inquiry he was engaged in illegal insider trading in Marconi shares. As a direct result of the part played by wireless in rescuing *Titanic's* survivors Marconi share prices had rocketed. Isaacs was making a fortune on the side.

Captain Lord and his officers gave their evidence and were then allowed to go about their business. After they had left the inquiry, in direct contravention of the principles of justice, the initial list of questions the inquiry was to answer was altered specifically to allow the court to lay the blame at Lord's door for the loss of life when *Titanic* sank.

When Lord Mersey made his report, published on 31 July, it was apparent that the inquiry, just like its American counterpart, had failed to find the cause of the disaster. The best that Mersey could manage was that the ship had been navigated at excessive speed and a proper watch had not been kept, the ship's boats had been

S.S. "MACKAY BENNETT" RECOVERY SHIP OF S.S. "TITANIC" "DROWNED"

*Left:* Shortly after the sinking of the *Titanic* the White Star Line chartered a series of ships, *Mackay Bennett*, *Minia* and *Montmagny*, to search for any bodies floating in the sea. The first of these, the cable ship *Mackay Bennett*, recovered a total of 306 corpses, buoyed up by their lifejackets.

*Below:* Of the 306 bodies recovered by *Mackay Bennett* 116 were so badly mutilated that they were identified wherever possible and then buried at sea. The remaining 190 were brought back to Halifax, just over half of them in plain pine coffins and the rest wrapped in canvas. The corpses were laid out at Halifax's Mayflower Ice Rink, which served as an impromptu mortuary, where they could be identified and claimed by relatives. The remainder were buried in the town's three principal cemeteries. The picture shows extra coffins, for *Titanic's* victims, awaiting the arrival of *Mackay Bennett*, at Halifax.

HALIFAX NOVA SCOTIA. S.S. "TITANIC" DEAD ON QUAYSIDE.

properly lowered but not properly manned, the track taken by the ship would have been safe if a proper watch had been kept, and that third class passengers had not been discriminated against. In every respect, except that of the boats being improperly manned, the report was wrong. Everything else about the voyage had been normal everyday practice.

The Mersey inquiry was not a court of law and had no right to determine guilt on anybody's part, but the report devotes 3½ closely typed pages to condemning Captain Lord. According to Lord Mersey's inquiry, *Californian* might have reached *Titanic* if she had attempted to do so. Captain Smith, J. Bruce Ismay and Sir Cosmo Duff Gordon were all exonerated.

Captain Lord was relieved of his command even though the owners of the *Californian* did not believe him to be guilty of failing to respond to a distress signal. Within a very short time he was given command of a larger vessel belonging to another line with no apparent connection to I.M.M. Although he asked to be charged with the crime specified in the Mersey report, his request was denied. Captain Lord was effectively found guilty without trial and without any chance to defend himself. He fought the injustice till the end of his life.

Dr Robert Ballard's discovery of the wreck in 1985, finally establishing the exact position of *Titanic* when she sank, proved that the inquiry's findings were as wrong about Captain Lord as they were about almost everything else.

Some good came out of the Mersey inquiry. From that time forward all passenger ships would carry enough lifeboats to ensure, should the worst happen, that there were pre-allocated seats for all aboard, and there would be regular lifeboat drills. All passenger ships were also required from then on to carry wireless sets manned for 24 hours a day.

And, of course, the sound and fury of the two official government inquiries had deflected public attention from the real causes of the disaster and focused it on Captain Lord and the *Californian*.

## Red Star Line Steamer LAPLAND

Length : 620 feet. Tonnage : 18,694.

*Above:* **The Red Star liner *Lapland*, which delivered *Titanic's* surviving ordinary crew-members into temporary captivity at Plymouth.**

*Left:* **Plymouth, where *Titanic's* crew-members were held, interrogated and sworn to secrecy, before being allowed to return to their homes.**

The Hoe Promenade Pier, Plymouth.

202.

T.S. "Lapland."

*Above: Lapland,* which brought most of *Titanic's* surviving ordinary crew-members back to Britain.

*Right:* Liverpool Landing Stage, where *Titanic's* surviving officers arrived back in England. Unlike the ordinary crew-members they do not appear to have been de-briefed or threatened with the Official Secrets Act.

The Landing Stage, Liverpool

*Above: Adriatic,* the vessel which brought Joseph Bruce Ismay back to England after the farcical American inquiry into the loss of the *Titanic*.

*Below: Adriatic* approaching the landing stage at Liverpool, where J. Bruce Ismay left the ship ready to face the British inquiry.

*Left:* The palm court and restaurant of *Majestic*. Passengers booked for *Titanic's* second or subsequent voyages were hardly being obliged to 'rough it'.

*Below:* Friends and relatives of *Titanic's* crew wait outside the line's Southampton offices for news, some of them for up to a fortnight. Most of the crew came from Southampton and hardly a street escaped loss.

The Most Appalling Disaster in Maritime History.
The White Star Liner "TITANIC," sunk on her maiden voyage off Cape Race, 15th April, 1912.

E ICEBERGS

*Above:* Postcard manufacturers were not slow in capitalising on the disaster and commemorative cards proliferated. Most of the earliest, derived from advertising material, showed *Olympic* instead of *Titanic*.

*Left:* The same image of *Olympic* masquerading as *Titanic* as shown above but artistically altered to show the ship passing through a field of ice.

R.M.S. "Oceanic"

R. M. S. Majestic,

White Star Liner "Titanic."
Left Southampton on maiden voyage, April 10th, 1912.
Collided with icefield and sank, Monday, 15th April.
Length, 882 feet ; beam, 92 feet ; tonnage, 46,192
Captain, E. J. Smith.

*Above left: Oceanic*, on which Mrs Florence Ismay sailed to intercept her husband, J. Bruce Ismay, at Queenstown on his return to Britain following the disaster.

*Left: Majestic*, which took over *Titanic's* duties following the loss of the White Star Line's flagship. The White Star tender *Magnetic* is alongside.

*Above:* Another card showing *Olympic* as *Titanic*. This one adds to the confusion by listing the vessel's tonnage as 46,192, which is incorrect for either ship.

*Right:* A memorial postcard derived from the previous example. This card at least was produced with the best of intentions and proceeds from its sale went to the *Titanic* disaster relief fund.

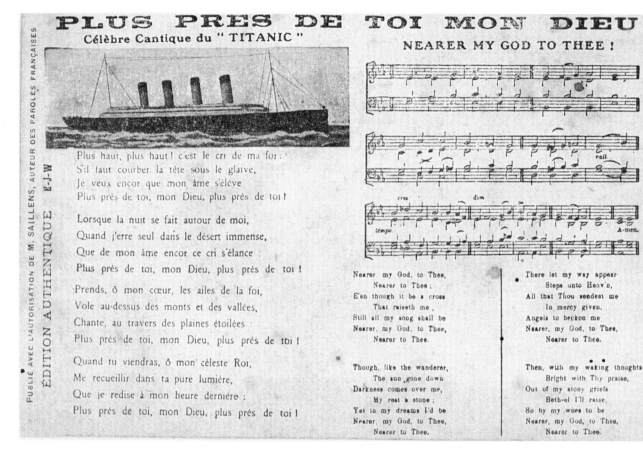

PUBLIÉ AVEC L'AUTORISATION DE M. SAILLENS, AUTEUR DES PAROLES FRANÇAISES — ÉDITION AUTHENTIQUE E-J-W

## PLUS PRÈS DE TOI MON DIEU !

Célèbre Cantique du " TITANIC "

### NEARER MY GOD TO THEE !

Plus haut, plus haut ! c'est le cri de ma foi :
S'il faut courber la tête sous le glaive,
Je veux encor que mon âme s'élève
Plus près de toi, mon Dieu, plus près de toi !

Lorsque la nuit se fait autour de moi,
Quand j'erre seul dans le désert immense,
Que de mon âme encor ce cri s'élance :
Plus près de toi, mon Dieu, plus près de toi !

Prends, ô mon cœur, les ailes de la foi,
Vole au-dessus des monts et des vallées,
Chante, au travers des plaines étoilées :
Plus près de toi, mon Dieu, plus près de toi !

Quand tu viendras, ô mon céleste Roi,
Me recueillir dans ta pure lumière,
Que je redise à mon heure dernière :
Plus près de toi, mon Dieu, plus près de toi !

Nearer, my God, to Thee,
Nearer to Thee;
E'en though it be a cross
That raiseth me,
Still all my song shall be
Nearer, my God, to Thee,
Nearer to Thee.

Though, like the wanderer,
The sun gone down,
Darkness comes over me,
My rest a stone;
Yet in my dreams I'd be
Nearer, my God, to Thee,
Nearer to Thee.

There let my way appear
Steps unto Heav'n,
All that Thou sendest me
In mercy given,
Angels to beckon me
Nearer, my God, to Thee,
Nearer to Thee.

Then, with my waking thoughts
Bright with Thy praise,
Out of my stony griefs
Beth-el I'll raise,
So by my woes to be
Nearer, my God, to Thee,
Nearer to Thee.

Format In-8°, prix O 35. — Grand format, 1 fr. net, comprenant la musique de la version Française. Henry WYÉIS, Éditeur, 166. Rue Montmartre. Paris. Tous droits réservés.

White Star Royal Mail Steamer "Titanic".
Tonnage 45000 tons, Length 882½ feet, Breadth 92½ feet.

*Above:* A French commemorative card with the words of 'Nearer My God To Thee' in English. The ship shown is again *Olympic*.

*Left: Titanic* commemorative card with a painting of *Olympic*. *By kind permission of Philip Croucher of Rembrandt.*

*Above right:* American card with *Olympic* labelled as *Titanic*. This card, derived from an earlier advertisement, has *Titanic* at left steaming away.

*Right:* Another American card with *Olympic* standing in for *Titanic*.

**"STEAMER TITANIC"**
Largest and most luxurious in the
World. Launched at Belfast Ireland,
May 1911. Length 882 ft. 6 inches.
Displacement 66,000 tons.
On her maiden trip struck
a mammoth iceberg on
Sunday, April 14th at 10.25 P. M.
41º 46 minutes, north
latitude-50º 14 minutes,
west longitude.
The worst disaster known
in Marine History.
Sunk at 2.20 A. M.
April 15 1912, with
a loss of over
1500 lives.

**"STEAMER TITANIC"**
Largest and most luxurious in the World. Launched at Belfast Ireland, May 1911. Length 882 ft. 6 in. Displacement
66,000 tons. On her maiden trip struck a mammoth iceberg on Sunday, April 14th at 10.25 P. M. in 41º 49 minutes,
north latitude-50º 14 minutes, West longitude. The worst disaster known in Marine History. Sunk at 2.20 A. M.
April 15 1912, with a loss of over 1300 lives.

THE S. S. "TITANIC"; 882 ft. long; the largest ship in the world; sunk April 15, 1912, at 2:20 A. M.; on her maiden trip; with a loss of about 1635 passengers.

White Star triple-screw steamer "Titanic" 45,000 tons, which sank on April 15th 1912 with 1635 people.

"ADCO" Series.

# R.M.S. TITANIC IN MID-OCEAN

*Above left: Olympic* riding at anchor. *Titanic's* name has been added at the bow in somewhat oversized lettering.

*Left: Olympic* at Liverpool on 1 June 1911.

*Above:* Artistic rendition of *Olympic* in choppy seas, again identified as *Titanic*. To the untutored eye the sisters were indistinguishable from one another.

*Right:* Joseph C. Nichols, a second class passenger who went down with the ship.

IN LOVING MEMORY
OF
*Joseph C. Nicholls*
(THE BELOVED SON OF RICHARD H.
AND AGNES NICHOLLS)
WHO LOST HIS LIFE IN THE
TITANIC DISASTER
APRIL 15, 1912
AGED 19 YEARS, 8 MONTHS
*Gone to be with Jesus which is far better*

*Right, top to bottom:*

Commemorative card actually showing *Titanic*, and perpetuating the myth of Captain Smith's last words, 'Be British'. Captain Smith was on the bridge of *Titanic* during the latter part of the sinking.

Another card showing *Titanic* and quoting Captain Smith's supposed last words. What little evidence there is regarding Smith's actions during the latter part of the sinking suggests that he was overcome by the enormity of the situation, for which he was ultimately responsible, and had retired to the bridge in a state of shock.

This card not only shows the ship and Captain Smith but also pays tribute to some of the real heroes aboard *Titanic*. The ship's band played right to the end in an effort to calm passengers, with no thought of their own safety.

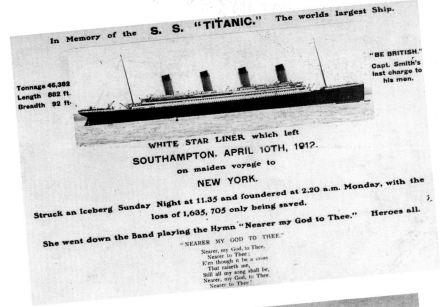

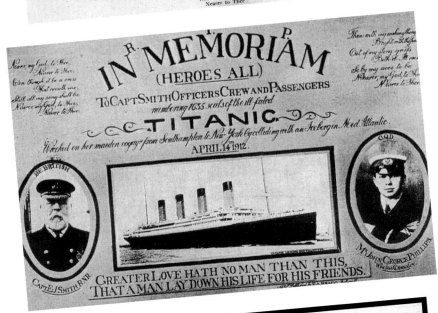

110

TITANIC DISASTER APRIL 15TH 1912
1,635 PERISH AT SEA

① CAPTAIN SMITH. ② PHILLIPS, THE HERO OPERATOR.
3. RESCUING A PASSENGER.

*Above:* An artistic representation of the sinking, again showing Captain Smith and the ship. John (Jack) George Phillips, the senior wireless operator is also featured. Phillips, unlike his junior, was still at his post trying to summon aid when the ship foundered.

*Left:* Many cards were produced showing the words and music of the last hymn played aboard *Titanic* moments before she foundered. The picture is of *Titanic* setting out from Southampton at the start of her voyage into notoriety.

**THE ILL-FATED WHITE STAR LINER "TITANIC"**
Struck an iceberg off the coast of Newfoundland on her maiden voyage and sunk with over One Thousand Six Hundred of her Passengers and Crew, Monday Morning, April 15th, 1912.

**NEARER, MY GOD, TO THEE.**

Nearer, my God, to Thee,
    Nearer to Thee;
E'en though it be a cross
    That raiseth me;
Still all my song shall be
Nearer, my God, to Thee,
    Nearer, to Thee.

Though like the wanderer,
    The sun gone down,
Darkness comes over me,
    My rest a stone;
Yet in my dreams I'd be
Nearer, my God, to Thee,
    Nearer to Thee.

There let my way appear
    Steps unto Heav'n.
All that Thou sendest me
    in mercy given,
Angels to beckon me
Nearer, my God, to Thee,
    Nearer to Thee.

Then, with my waking thoughts
    Bright with Thy praise,
Out of my stony griefs
    Beth-el I'll raise;
So by my woes to be
Nearer, my God, to Thee,
    Nearer to Thee.

**The Hymn to the strains of which the "Titanic" sunk.**

111

WOVEN IN SILK

R.M.S. TITANIC.

*Left:* A commemorative card woven in silk but showing *Titanic's* slightly older sister. The two vessels were constantly being confused at the time.

*Below left:* Another very unusual card commemorating the loss of the liner. This card, more than any other, brings home the enormity of the disaster. Although it is perhaps a little crude, this card was home made, almost certainly by a child who had lost someone in the sinking.

*Below:* A variation on a theme. Captain Smith, the words and music to 'Nearer My God To Thee', and a picture of *Olympic*.

*Right:* A French commemorative card showing an unknown vessel with *Titanic's* name on the bow. The vessel appears to be flying an unusual variety of national flags with the French tricolour at the bow, the American Stars and Stripes on the foremast, an indeterminate flag on the mainmast and the British Union Flag at the stern. In 1912 only ships built in America were entitled to fly the Stars and Stripes. *By kind permission of Philip Croucher of Rembrandt.*

*Below right:* An unusually clear view of *Titanic* in this commemorative card.

TITANIC

S.S. "TITANIC."

LENGTH, 882 FEET; BEAM, 92 FEET; TONNAGE, 46,192.

COLLIDED WITH ICEBERG

ON MAIDEN VOYAGE, 15th APRIL, 1912

CAPTAIN EDWARD J. SMITH, R.N.R.

NEARER MY GOD TO THEE!

Hymn played by Bandsmen of the S.S. "TITANIC" as she sank to her doom, 15th April, 1912.

Le "TITANIC" jaugeant 45.000 tonnes, longueur 288 m. 977, largeur 28 m. 193, profondeur 29 m. 66, a coûté 46 millions. Coulé à 3.200 mètres de fond dans la traversée de Southampton à New-York à la suite d'un abordage avec un bloc de glace. 1.800 victimes — 16 Avril 1912

### "TITANIC"
#### THE LARGEST SHIP IN THE WORLD,
WRECKED ON HER MAIDEN VOYAGE FROM SOUTHAMPTON TO NEW YORK, COLLIDING WITH AN ICEBERG IN MID-ATLANTIC WITH 1635 SOULS, APRIL 15, 1912.

White Star Liner "TITANIC."

Left Southampton on maiden voyage, April 10th, 1912.
Collided with icefield and sank, Monday, 15th April.

Length, 882 feet; beam, 92 feet; tonnage, 46,192.

Captain, E. J. Smith.

Nearer, my God, to Thee, Nearer to Thee!
E'en though it be a cross that raiseth me;
Still all my song shall be,
Nearer, my God, to Thee, Nearer to Thee!

"Save, Lord, we perish," was their cry,
"O save us in our agony!"
Thy word above the storm rose high
"Peace, be still."

*Left:* Another card sold in aid of the *Titanic* disaster fund, showing *Olympic*.

*Below left and this page:* Some memorial cards were very well produced, as this set of six by Bamforths, which all show a fairly accurate depiction of *Titanic's* last moments.

*Above left:* Officers from White Star vessels marching to the *Titanic* memorial service held at St Mary's Church, Southampton, on 20 April 1912. *By kind permission of Philip Croucher of Rembrandt.*

*Left:* Mourners crowd into St Mary's Church, Southampton, for the memorial service for those lost with *Titanic*. *By kind permission of Philip Croucher of Rembrandt.*

*Above:* Wallace Hartley's hearse and coffin, followed by the funeral procession passing the town hall of his home town, Colne, in Lancashire.

*Right:* Hartley's funeral procession passing his one-time home at 90 Albert Road, Colne, on its mile-long journey from funeral parlour to cemetery. Approximately 40,000 mourners turned out for Hartley's funeral, to pay tribute to one of the real heroes of the *Titanic* disaster.

WALLACE
HARTLEY

BANDMASTER OF
THE R.M.S TITANIC
WHO PERISHED IN
THE FOUNDERING
OF THAT VESSEL
APRIL 15TH 1912.

ERECTED BY VOLUNTARY
CONTRIBUTIONS TO COM-
MEMORATE THE HEROISM
OF A NATIVE OF THIS
TOWN

*Left:* The Wallace
Hartley memorial at
Colne, Lancashire.

*Above:* The Hartley family grave at
Colne Cemetery where Wallace Hartley
was interred with his parents and
brothers.

*Left:* The grave of *Titanic's* lookout
Frederick Fleet, who tried so
desperately to avert the disaster. Fleet
apparently hanged himself in 1965.
He was originally buried in a pauper's
grave until this incredibly tasteless
memorial stone was erected by the
American *Titanic* Historical Society.
As if Fred Fleet needs to be reminded
throughout eternity that he was a
lookout on duty aboard *Titanic* at the
time of the collision that caused the
vessel to founder with the loss of more
than 1,500 lives.

*Left:* The grave of Captain Arthur Rostron whose actions on the night of 14/15 April 1912 resulted in the saving of 705 people from *Titanic*. Captain Rostron died in 1940 and his wife, Ethel, joined him three years later. At the time the gravestone was erected nobody saw any necessity to record Captain Rostron's part in the *Titanic* disaster — the inscription at the base of the stone is a later addition. Unfortunately, whoever defaced the gravestone failed to take notice of what Captain Rostron had insisted was the number of *Titanic* survivors he and the rest of the crew of the *Carpathia* had rescued: 705.

*Below:* Liverpool's almost anonymous *Titanic* memorial soon after it was erected outside Liverpool's Liver Building. The memorial has no inscription because, allegedly, White Star Line officials believed that reminders of what had happened to *Titanic* might frighten off potential passengers..

LIVER, CUNARD, AND DOCK OFFICES, LIVERPOOL.

*Left:* The *Titanic* memorial in Belfast, at the side of the City Hall.

*Below: Titanic* Engineers' Memorial at Southampton, as it appeared in 1915.

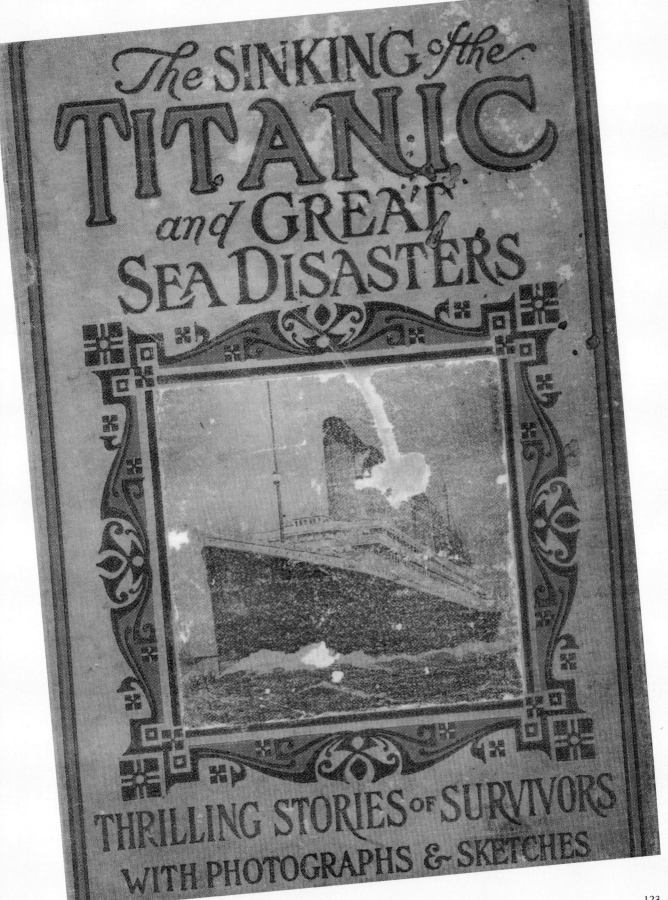

The SINKING of the TITANIC and GREAT SEA DISASTERS

THRILLING STORIES OF SURVIVORS

WITH PHOTOGRAPHS & SKETCHES

The DEATHLESS STORY
OF THE
TITANIC

COMPLETE
NARRATIVE
WITH MANY
ILLUSTRATIONS

2ᴰ

Other accounts did strive for accuracy, such as this rather
unfortunately named special by *Lloyd's Weekly News*, written
by Phillip Gibbs, and priced at 2d.

# AFTERWORD

The story of the *Titanic* as related in this book may not follow the course expected by the reader as the authors believe that the ship which sank on 15 April 1912 was not RMS *Titanic* but her slightly older and almost identical sister ship, RMS *Olympic*. The ships were switched because of a collision, in September 1911, between *Olympic* and the Royal Navy's armoured cruiser HMS *Hawke*, in which both vessels were seriously damaged. As a result of this collision, *Olympic* required two months of repair at her builders, Harland & Wolff at Belfast, before she could apparently resume her normal duties as a first-class transatlantic liner. During the time the liner was out of action she cost her owners, the White Star Line, more than a quarter of a million pounds in repair bills and lost fares. At the end of the two-month repair *Olympic* was still not fit to resume her duties but with her at the builders was the almost completed *Titanic*. What more natural course of action could there be, in an effort to recoup some of the lost earnings, than to send the untested *Titanic* to sea in her sister's place?

Having once allowed *Titanic* to take *Olympic's* place, the owners were left with a seriously damaged ship that they had somehow to pass off as new. Changing name plates, giving the vessel a new coat of paint and replacing any damaged fixtures and fittings would have been child's play for the builders, but the structural damage to the ship's hull was a different kettle of fish. No matter what they did, the ship would always carry the effects of the collision, if only in as much as she could not again be trimmed to float on an even keel. As *Titanic*, *Olympic* always exhibited an unyielding tendency to list to port, which advertised her true identity.

By the time it became apparent that *Olympic* could not be passed off as the new *Titanic* in the long term, the White Star Line management's options had become somewhat limited. They could tell the truth and face the music for allowing *Titanic*, a vessel with no Board of Trade certificates for safety or seaworthiness, to carry emigrants and other fare-paying passengers and allow both ships to return to their true identities, or they could get rid of the *Olympic* once and for all. They chose the second option, which had the merits of allowing them to collect a considerable sum in insurance money and of keeping them out of prison for having switched the ship's identities in the first place.

Having decided to dispose of *Olympic*, as *Titanic*, the senior executives of White Star, its parent company the International Mercantile Marine Co, and Harland & Wolff, needed a plan. Given the resources available to them it did not take long to decide on a course of action. *Olympic*, as *Titanic*, would be sailed out into the middle of the Atlantic Ocean as if on a normal voyage. Once into the deepest water available, they would simulate a collision with an iceberg. All of the people aboard the liner would be taken off by other IMM vessels which would be in the area, standing by. Then the sea cocks of the liner would be opened and she would quietly sink. Had the plan worked, the name of the *Titanic* would now be long forgotten, but the plan did not work.

Everything went well until the night of 14 April 1912. The already unserviceable ship had behaved herself reasonably well, despite her list and the vibration coming from her engines. Then, at soon after 11pm, in the middle of a huge icefield that the ship's officers were all too aware was there, it all went horribly wrong. Whether the ship actually struck an iceberg or another ship is unclear, and for all practical purposes immaterial, but she ran into something despite the best efforts of the lookouts to warn the officers on the bridge that something lay in the vessel's path. Only at the last moment did the officer effectively in command of *Titanic* at that time react to the lookout's warnings by turning the ship's bows towards the south, away from where a primary rescue vessel lay waiting. In that helm order, 'hard-a-starboard', issued by First Officer Murdoch, lay the death warrants of more than 1,500 people aboard the ship.

Instead of just pretending, *Titanic* really was sinking, and she was not where the prearranged rescue ships expected to find her; nor was she sinking at the time they expected to go to the rescue of those aboard. Other ships did try to reach the sinking liner in response to her wirelessed distress calls but most of them were too far away to get there in time. Unfortunately for many of those aboard *Titanic*, a vessel intended to take them off was a little way to their north, just too far away to see their distress rockets, and with her wireless operator tucked snugly up in bed. They would know nothing of the disaster before the following morning.

For a more detailed account of the switch and subsequent sinking of the *Titanic* the authors recommend you read the book *Titanic: The Ship That Never Sank?* by Robin Gardiner (published by Ian Allan Publishing).

# INDEX

**Illustrations shown in bold.**

Titles in brackets apply to *Titanic* unless otherwise stated.